WOMEN RESISTING SEXUAL VIOLENCE AND THE EGYPTIAN REVOLUTION

ABOUT THE AUTHOR

Manal Hamzeh is a Professor of Gender and Sexualities at the Department of Interdisciplinary Studies of New Mexico State University. Dr. Hamzeh's teaching and research draw on antiracist educational theories and decolonial feminist research methodologies. She is the author of *Pedagogies of Deveiling* (2012) and co-writer of the short animation film *The Four Hijabs* (2016), with playwright Jamil Khoury of Chicago's Silk Road Rising Theater.

WOMEN RESISTING SEXUAL VIOLENCE AND THE EGYPTIAN REVOLUTION

Arab Feminist Testimonies

Manal Hamzeh

I.B. TAURIS

LONDON • NEW YORK • OXFORD • NEW DELHI • SYDNEY

I.B. TAURIS
Bloomsbury Publishing Plc
50 Bedford Square, London, WC1B 3DP, UK
1385 Broadway, New York, NY 10018, USA
29 Earlsfort Terrace, Dublin 2, Ireland

BLOOMSBURY, I.B. TAURIS and the I.B. Tauris logo
are trademarks of Bloomsbury Publishing Plc

First published in Great Britain 2020
This paperback edition published 2022

ISBN: HB: 978-1-7869-9621-3
PB: 978-1-3503-3332-1
ePDF: 978-1-7869-9622-0
eBook: 978-1-7869-9623-7
mobi: 978-1-7869-9624-4

Typeset by Jones Ltd, London

To find out more about our authors and books visit
www.bloomsbury.com and sign up for our newsletters.

To Samira Ibrahim, Yasmine El Baramawy, and Ola Shahba, who trusted me with their shahadat, and to all the Egyptian women who made suwret yanayer happen.

CONTENTS

ACKNOWLEDGMENTS

I write here with sincere appreciation for those I love and respect, who have been generous with their collaborations and conversations with me over eight years. Those are many; first and foremost, the three women at the center of this book, Samira Ibrahim, Yasmine El Baramawy, and Ola Shahba. I have no more words, just appreciation and love for all the trust and kindness you shared with me. *Alf shukur.*

Special thanks to my dear friend Nadia Kamel. You have been so generous with your insights, home, food, and insightful conversations. Thank you to my cousin, Yassar, for keeping Cairo as a home and Egyptian dialect close

Huda Elsadda and Faiha Abdulhadi, thank you for your femtoring and your powerful Arab feminist scholarship.

With love, gratitude, and respect for years of friendship, the struggles of maintaining solidarity and negotiating imperial borders, and co-creating transborderly knowledges, thank you Cynthia Bejarano and Judith Flores Carmona.

Special thanks to Tabitha Parry Collins for their touches on the words and looks of the text. I am also thankful to Kim Walker at Zed Books for believing in this project and for her patience along the way.

Heather Sykes, I have no words for your unwavering understanding and limitless support. In return, I offer my humility, appreciation, and unconditional love.

1 | WOMEN'S RESISTANCE IN THE EGYPTIAN REVOLUTION: ARABYYA FEMINIST METHODOLOGIES

This book is about the resistance of three women who experienced state-sanctioned violence during the Egyptian Revolution. Egyptian women's shahadat [testimonios][1] worked as tools of resistance and also as powerful exposés about their major contributions to suwret yanayer.[2] Suwret yanayer is the Arabic term, which I use throughout the book, for the Egyptian January 25 Revolution of 2011. This Egyptian revolution was the monumental popular uprising in 2011 against the brutality of a police state and the oligarchy of President Hosni Mubarak.[3] On January 25, the first day, hundreds of thousands of people spontaneously took to the streets in "twenty different points in Cairo ... flooding the iconic Tahrir Square" (Bayat, 2017, p. 9), midan etahrir [Liberation Square].[4] In the following days, millions of people began protesting in other cities across Egypt. Protestors burned police stations and battled police forces who had tortured them for decades. They also fought the central security forces[5] who had repressed them for more than a generation. Women were in the streets and at the forefront of these protests from day one. Paul Amar asserted that though the Egyptians were inspired by Tunisia's uprising the month before, they were "also driven by Egypt's own homegrown wave of mass-scale labor, civic, feminist anti-police mobilization which had begun to emerge around the year 2000" (Amar, 2013, p. 25). In suwret yanayer, the Egyptian people demanded the end of Mubarak's regime, chanting "alsha'b yureed isqatt elnizam" [people want the downfall of the regime].[6] They also called for "'aish, huryya, 'adalah igtima'yya" [bread, freedom, and social justice].[7]

This book is built on the shahadat of three women who were protesting in the streets during suwret yanayer and who experienced state-sanctioned sexual violence during the power transition period after suwret yanayer, which occurred between 2011 and 2012. Three separate chapters present the shahadat of Samira Ibrahim's[8] experience of kushoof el'uzryyah [virginity inspections or virginity exposures][9] in March 2011, Yasmine El Baramawy's[10] experience of organized mob rape in November 2012, and Ola Shahba's[11] experience of detention and sexual assault in December 2012. Each chapter offers unprecedented full and direct access to the shahadat given shortly after the assaults. This is an exposé of the transitional regimes, the militarists and the Islamists. These regimes were against suwret yanayer and its goals, and against essuwar,[12] the revolutionists.

Each shahada [testimonio][13] was translated from oral Egyptian Arabic into English as a reconstructed "testimonial text" (Reyes & Rodríguez, 2012, p. 526). They foreground the words and theorizing of Egyptian women within a two-year period after the profound and complex moment of suwret yanayer. Importantly, the women who give testimonios of their complex bodily experiences, the shaahedat [testimonialistas][14] (Delgado Bernal et al., 2012), are at the center of this work.

The testimonial texts in this book make two main contributions: *preserving* and *representing* the powerful shahadat of women resisting state-sanctioned sexual violence after suwret yanayer. First, preserving the shahadat of suwret yanayer adds to ongoing efforts to archive the record of suwret yanayer from the revolutionists' and the people's perspectives (*Mada Masr*, 2018), rather than the perspectives of the regimes in power. Reviving and remembering this part of the Egyptian people's collective memory of suwret yanayer is crucial. It also stems from the insistence to own and disseminate *their* narrative of suwret yanayer from the perspective of those who made it and are still working for its values and goals.

The shahadat by Samira, Yasmine and Ola about state-sanctioned physical and sexual violence counter the erasures of women's contribution in suwret yanayer. Their narratives challenge the normative social gendering order. Specifically, they challenge the patriarchal oppressive power of anti-revolution forces, both militarist and Islamist, in 2011 and 2012. Their shahadat were, and still are, major interruptions to the current regime's propaganda machine that is hard at work trying to erase suwret yanayer, and particularly women's contribution to it. Hence, preserving these shahadat is an act of subversion that reflects Egyptians' insistence to continue their revolution, especially since the militarists took over Egypt in 2013 (D'Isidoro, 2019). Preserving these shahadat is an act of revolutionary resistance.

Second, as a nasawyya Arabyya [Arab feminist],[15] this book is my humble representation of Egyptian women's shahadat in 2011–2012. It is my attempt to foreground how Egyptian women, at least the shaahedat represented in this book, resisted repression and theorized their experiences of gendered violence as they were seeking social justice. My work draws upon the legacy of the waves of Egyptian women's movements and feminist activism (Kamal, 2016) of the past hundred years. It is a small contribution to the Arab feminist movements of the past hundred years that struggled against colonial oppression and racist narratives about Arabs and Arab women (Ahmed, 1992; Al-Hassan Golley, 2004; Badran, 2007; El Saadawi, 1998; El Said et al., 2015; Mernissi, 1991; Naber, 2011). It adds to the critical research of Arabyya and Egyptian feminists that refutes Western imperial feminists and global liberal media narratives about the Arab revolutions of 2011, and particularly about Egyptian women in suwret yanayer (Badran, 2011; Hasso & Salime, 2016; Naber, 2011).

I build on the work of Arab feminist academics who also expose the collusion of the corrupt Arab regimes with imperial powers (Elsadda, 2011) and the brilliant theorizing of many Arabyya and Egyptian feminist artists and writers who demonstrate how women and their ways of resistance in suwret yanayer have shaped a new gendered landscape in Egypt and the rest of the Arab world (aamiry-khasawnih, 2018; Al-Ali, 2014; El Said et al., 2015; Moghadam, 2013). This work also draws on Muslim feminists' rewriting and theorizing of Islamic history (Ahmed, 1992; Mernissi, 1997) and those who reclaim the authority to reread the Qur'an by women themselves (Hamzeh, 2012; Mernissi, 1991; Wadud, 1999). Particularly, I attend to what Hala Kamal (2016) calls the fourth wave of Egyptian feminism, which focuses on "struggles into the realms of women's bodies and sexuality" (p. 4). At the same time, I engage calls by poststructural Arab feminists to attend to gendered bodies and their powerful capacities (Abouelnaga, 2016; Al-Nakib, 2013).

Hence, the three shahadat I represent in this book are examples of Arabyya methodologies that both represent *and* theorize women's bodily experiences of sexual violence and resistance. The shahadat of Samira, Yasmine, and Ola call feminists to pay attention to Egyptian women's shahadat as methodologies of resistance, healing, resilience, and imagination of a just Egypt. Samira, Yasmine, and Ola legitimize shahadat both as an Arabyya feminist methodology and as on-the-ground theorizing of resistance to gendered violence.

Before discussing the actual study that resulted in this book, I map my reasons for using Arabic names for the Egyptian Revolution of 2011, and then briefly review the latest nasawyya Arabyya rethinking of gender during the multiple Arab uprisings since 2011.

Naming the 2011 Egyptian Revolution

The Egyptians themselves refer to the 2011 Revolution using four main names interchangeably:

suwret yanayer [the January Revolution];

suwret khamsah ou 'ishreen yanayer [the January 25 Revolution];[16]

el ttamntta'shar yaum [the 18 Days];[17]

essuwra [the Revolution].[18]

All four names refer to the 18 days of massive Egyptian presence on the streets that began on January 25, 2011, with protests against police brutality on yaum eshurttah [Police Day],[19] and continued until February 11, when the dictator-president Hosni Mubarak was forced to resign (Bayat, 2017). The people named the day they succeeded in deposing Mubarak the "Day of Tanahhi" [stepping down or abdicating power].[20]

At the same time, essuwra was used to mark the beginning of a longer period of mass protests and the dynamic process of transition that lasted two more years from February 2011 to June 2012. This period includes the takeover of elmagles ela'la lilqwat almusalaha [the Supreme Council of the Armed Forces (SCAF)][21] to the election of a majority-Islamist parliament in December 2011 to the election of Mohammad Morsi as president, also an Islamist from the gama'et al ikhwan al muslimeen [Muslim Brotherhood],[22] in June 2012. A few days after Mubarak was ousted, the name evolved to essuwra mustamirah [the revolution continues or is continuous].[23] This term reflected how Egyptians maintained their civil disobedience, protests, and campaigning in the streets and squares of Egypt. They sustained their activism, and kept demanding radical changes to the governing regime and calling for the goals of suwret yanayer—"'aish, huryya, 'adalah igtima'yya" [bread, freedom, and social justice].

The overt state of living in and continuing essuwra almost stopped with the military abduction of Mohammed Morsi in June 2012 and the election of the military general Abdel Fattah El Sisi as president in July 2013. However, Egyptians have been in a state of revolution much longer than 18 days in 2011 and the two years after the ousting of Mubarak. According to Egyptian historian Khaled Fahmy (2015), revolution is not a new state of being for Egyptians and suwret yanayer is deeply rooted in Egypt's modern history. It is a continuation of not less than seven major rebellions and uprisings during a 200-year period of Egypt's modern history (Fahmy, 2015). This 2011 Revolution is also the extension of the "18 days," and what Paul Amar (2013) asserted as the deepening revolutionary processes ensuring "that Egypt's uprisings, over the long-term, will be seen to constitute a revolutionary dynamic" (p. 25). Suwret yanayer, in this case, is continuous and "still resists any kind of closure" (Mostafa, 2015, p. 118) It set the revolutionary dynamics in motion, the consequences of which won't be explicit or immediate (Mostafa, 2015).

In this nasawyya Arabyya study, I have four aims in deploying the Arabic terms Egyptians use(d) to describe their January 25 Revolution, as well as highlight essuwra mustamirah. First, this move defies superficial and erroneous descriptions of the 18 days that support the narratives of the powerful elites, which are channeled through major Western-established and Saudi-controlled media outlets. It also counters reductive depictions of uprisings in several Arab countries when they are all lumped under one term as "the Arab Spring." Though, as Amar and Prashad (2013) note, I recognize the "currency of the expression" (p. vii) Arab Spring, I also agree with them about its limitations for excluding revolutions of non-Arab populations, such as the Amazigh.

Second, using the Egyptian Arabic terms to refer to suwret yanayer, I emphasize the need to historicize and contextualize this complex action of millions of people. Through the monolithic lens of the "Arab Spring," the global mainstream liberal media, as well as Orientalist and/or imperial Western feminist academics, reduce this revolution to a short-lived phenomenon void of context and history (Abouelnaga, 2016). These media sources and academics reduced Egyptian women to "first-timers" in the political scene in Egypt and to its revolutions. They were even reluctant to consider them free-willed women, but instead still as helpless beings oppressed by Islam. Moreover, they robbed different Arabs from their history of struggle, the particularities of their context, and intricate circumstances as they rebelled in 2011. They represented suwret yanayer as a simple reaction to the Tunisian Revolution and the only inspiration to the people in Yemen, Libya, Bahrain, and Syria.

This simplified conception of different multilayered Arab revolutions was also built on the visual sensationalization of the 18 days in midan etahrir (Abouelnaga, 2016). The Egyptians themselves were continually misrepresented in isolation of a vast geographical area, colonially constructed and named "the Middle East." This disconnects from global interlocking structures of power, in this case the U.S.-supported imperial and neoliberal violent practice in Egypt (Naber & Said, 2016) backed up by Israel and Saudi Arabia. It is a classical construction of an imperial, outsider's gaze and voyeurism of Arabs.

Third, the use of the people's terms also respects the Egyptians themselves and their Egyptian Arabic language. It is a move in which I am insisting on the people's naming of their own revolution and calling for a closer look at their perspectives, voices, language, lived experiences, and struggles. Hence, with this move, I intended to create a space to listen to Egyptian scholars and activists on the ground. It is also a move to highlight the marginalized or the subalterns' sense-making about the context, setbacks, continuation, and impacts of essuwra while simultaneously living in overt, and sometimes covert, states of rebellion.

Fourth, my main analytic approach for this study is a transnational feminist translation, a political act and praxis of solidarity (Castro & Ergun, 2017). This is a form of dissenting in translation and "translating dissent" (Baker, 2016). Hence, my use of revolution-centered Arabic has the potential to open the space for

readers to leave English as the presumptive framework of thinking and lay out the "map of learning across linguistic distance and
forging ties of solidarity across different kinds of vocabularies and
frameworks" (Butler, cited in Castro & Ergun, 2017, p. 123).[24]

Next, I will review the latest Arab and Egyptian feminist
rethinking of gender during and after the Arab revolutions of
2010–2011 as another major part of the conceptual framing of
this book.

Rethinking Gender in Revolutionary Egypt

Research published by Arabyya and Egyptian feminists after
suwret yanayer has deepened our understanding of Egyptian
women's experiences and led to a rethinking about gender in
times of revolutions and resistance (Abouelnaga, 2016; Al-Ali,
2012; Alexander & Bassiouny, 2014; al-Natour, 2012; El-Mahdi
& Marfleet, 2009; El Said et al., 2015; Hasso & Salime, 2016).
This Arabyya research has thoroughly shown how Egyptian
women's revolutionary embodied experiences were not merely
visual static representations, but that they are at the core of
shaping a new gendered landscape in Egypt and the rest of the
Arab world. They also made clear that the bodies of Egyptian
women were both central sites of state violence and revolutionary resistance and resilience.

For instance, El Said et al. (2015) assert that there were
"different modalities of [Egyptian] women's agency" (p. 8) in
shaping the sociopolitical transformations of the revolutionary
moment. The revolutionary moment of suwret yanayer made
"gender reconstruction" (Abouelnaga, 2015, p.35) possible,
and new gender constructs were unfolding in the "18 days"
and as the Revolution continued. With the beginning of suwret
yanayer, women in public spaces were defying the Mubarak
regime's stunts against women's rights. Abouelnaga (2015)
emphasized how "the malleability of gendered subjectivities in
times of revolutions/resistance" (p. 36) was very apparent in the
post-January 25 Revolution context.

Many of the above studies, conducted after the ousting of Mubarak, focused on textual or visual material about suwret yanayer (Abouelnaga, 2016; Al-Ali, 2012; Alexander & Bassiouny, 2014; al-Natour, 2012; El-Mahdi & Marfleet, 2009; El Said et al., 2015; Hasso & Salime, 2016), while some centered on the oral narrative using interviews (Hassan & Magdy, 2018). Despite this important research, there is still limited access to women's experiences of essuwra and their critical reflections at this very complex and still dynamic moment. To fill this gap, I suggest that Arab feminists explore women's shahadat as an alternative methodology (Hamzeh, 2018). This responds to Egyptian scholars Hoda Elsadda and Hanan Sabea's (2018) call to:

> open the space for alternative practices of relating, practicing, and experiencing knowledge ... of recognizing events and non-events, of revealing fleeting ephemeral experiences, of recognizing the mundane and the ordinary as inseparable from the making of history, and of hailing different actors in the production of the political and of history. (p. 10)

I further suggest that there is a need to invite data using methodologies that are committed to building trust relationships with women on the ground to deepen our thinking about gendered subjectivities within revolutionary contexts. This book is a humble start to fill a gap.

Next I will briefly situate this study within nasawwya Arabyya, transnational, and Chicana feminist epistemologies. Then I will discuss the methodologies that guided this study, the profiles of each of the three women, the background to state gender violence in Egypt, three incidents of the main shahadat, data sources, and the data analysis process.

Intersecting Feminist Epistemologies

In this study, I drew on three intersecting theories: Arabyya, Chicana, and transnational feminist epistemologies. All three epistemologies are rooted in people's revolutions and struggles against colonialism, militarism, patriarchy, imperial borders, religious institutions, genocide, land theft, capitalism, and racism within specific histories and contexts.

First, Arabyya epistemologies are at the center of this study. As an Arabyya-centered study, it is anchored in the politics of dissent and committed to the traditions of theorizing gendered experiences of oppression in the lives of Arabic-speaking people and the context they live and history they have lived. Arabyya epistemologies focus on reading the contexts of Arabic-speaking peoples and their long struggle against British and French colonialisms and Zionist-Israeli settler-colonialism. I describe Arabyya epistemologies as the knowledges and theorizing of Arab women's lived experiences during their 100 years of struggle against Western coloniality. This includes their resistance to the perpetual wars and occupations by imperial powers, settler-colonial theft of Palestine, and the militarized and Islamized postcolonial dictatorships of all Arab-majority countries (Abdelhadi & Abdulhadi, 2002; Ahmed, 1992; El Saadawi, 1998; Mernissi, 1991). Arabyya epistemologies are focused on reading and resisting the intersecting nexus of militarism, neoliberalism and capitalism, Islamism, settler-colonialism, and heteronormativity oppressing the bodies of Arabs in different geographical contexts.

In the academy of North America, Arabyya epistemologies or Arab feminisms are not recognized as a field of study or even part of intersectional feminisms. Superficially, it may be understood as a new "women's liberation movement" and more often than not contested as an extension or a copy of "Western" feminism (Badran, 2009). Other times, alnasawyyat al arabyya [Arab feminisms][25] are labeled as "Middle Eastern" feminisms (Leavy & Harris, 2019, p. 89), Islamic feminisms, and at times Islamist feminisms (Badran, 2009).

My purpose in using the term "Arabyya" is to assert that Arab feminisms stand on their own—they are not borrowed or dictated to from the West (Badran, 2009). I want to assert a broader use of the term "Arabyya" and begin circulating it in the English-reading academy. I am deliberate in my use of the term "Arabyya" as a more inclusive and larger umbrella to alnasawyyat al Arabyya. This is to reflect a century-long unrecognized epistemology in a diverse and complex period of time and over a very large geographical area.

Moreover, my use of Arabic in this book is an intentional assertion that the knowledge co-created in this study is a core principle of Arab feminism. Using Arabic terms throughout this book is an Arabyya defiance to the dominance of English, as a colonialist language, in the academy of the Global North. At the same time, asserting the use of Arabyya is a way of bridging the work of transnational feminists across borders (Mohanty, 2013). This means that as I work in the U.S. academy bridging the research in the Arab world and with Arab women, I draw on transnational feminist notions and methodological practices of both "solidarities across borders" (Mohanty, 2013, p. 967) as well as "situated solidarities" (Nagar, 2014, Kindle location 279). I also draw on "the insurgent knowledges and the complex politics of antiracist, anti-imperial feminisms" (Mohanty, 2013, p. 987) and the new revolutionary women resisting on the frontlines in the Arab context. As such, I attend to the "specificities of geographical ... and to the particular combination of processes, events, and struggles underway in those locations" (Nagar, 2014, Kindle locations 279–281), hence my engagement with the Egyptian Revolution of 2011 within a larger context of revolutions in the Arab world.

Finally, bringing an Arabyya methodology to this project meant building and maintaining trust relationships, hence shaping this study as a solidarity-centered project in which those collaborating hear each other better. My Arabyya perspective also meant engaging feminist knowledges with Egyptian women within transborder and transnational social movements struggling against global capitalism, militarism, and imperialism (Mohanty, 2013). This methodology is meant to produce a praxis that is flexible, tactical, and contextual (Nagar, 2014). It was a methodology that unfolded within Arabyya collaborations and direct work with women in Egypt who live at the frontlines of essuwra.

As the main researcher and writer in this project, I also draw on connections between Arabyya and Chicana feminist thought as both are anti-colonial and critical feminist epistemologies. I am an Arab feminist scholar working in the U.S. academy located on the southwest Mexico–U.S. border at the heart of the U.S. Empire. I work closely with Chicanas fighting against the U.S. imperial colonial settler borders and the racist academy (Flores Carmona et al., 2018).

My ways of knowing are representative of epistemological solidarity between Arabyya and Chicanas. I build on the collaborations between Arab-American/Palestinian feminists and Chicanas (Abdelhadi & Abdulhadi, 2002). I also draw on Chicanas' praxis of theorizing from the flesh (Moraga, 2002), from the tradition of theorizing from the brown female body (Anzaldúa, 1999; Moraga & Anzaldúa, 2002), from the borders and in-between subjectivities (Anzaldúa, 1999), and from intuitive knowledges (Delgado Bernal, 1998). Given that I am always living in translation not only between Arabic and English, but also between my privileges as an academic and the painful visceral realities of borders, checkpoints, visas, and passports, I live in between languages and in between Arabyya and Chicana epistemologies with connected cross-border resistance and resilience.

In this solidarity with Chicanas, I learned how our anti-militarist, anti-imperial, and anti-patriarchal struggles are interconnected. As Arabyya and Chicana feminists of color here in the United States, we have a common commitment that is focused on the same nexus of power however it looks in different global locations. We are guided by the urgency to counter the violence in U.S. academies (Flores Carmona et al., 2018; Hamzeh & Flores Carmona, 2019). We are committed to the exposure of exploiting and trafficking women's bodies and labor. We are all up against the consolidated powers and dominance of masculinity/femininity, heteronormativity, racism, and nationalism (Flores Carmona et al., 2018; Hamzeh & Flores Carmona, 2019). We are deploying the commonalities and feeding each other to expose and resist the foundations of patriarchy in militarism, colonialism, and racism. Hence, the methodologies of this study are also informed by these interconnections between Arabyya and Chicana epistemologies.

Arabyya Methodologies of Shahadat and Haki

Two main Arabyya methodologies drove this four-year-long qualitative research project: shahadat and haki.[26] My own use of shahadat and haki emerged, and were named, through my collaboration with Chicanas who use the methodologies of testimonios and pláticas; however, they are also Arabyya methodologies par excellence. They have been grounded in the social and political traditions and struggles of Arab women against oppressive systems for decades and they are surely part of Arab methodologies of oral history (Abdulhadi, 2017). In one sense, shahadat have not really been recognized as a standalone Arabyya methodology.

In a huge oral history project about the Palestinians lives before and after 1948, Faiha Abdulhadi, Palestinian feminist, activist, poet, and scholar of oral history, captured the silenced and erased testimonies of mainly Palestinian women's activism the past century against British colonialism and the Zionist-Israeli state (Abdulhadi, 2006a, 2006b, 2009). More recently, efforts to collect shahadat during and after suwret yanayer was an everyday practice of activists, lawyers, journalists, and civic and human rights organizations, such as Mosireen Media Collective, El Nadeem, and Nazra for Feminist Studies. These shahadat were captured on video and disseminated online. Hence, I argue that as guides and tools of knowing, shahadat and haki were already used in Arab contexts during the revolts of the past century, albeit not named or recognized by academics as research methodologies. Nevertheless, Abdulhadi (2017) reminds us that Palestinians have used haki for decades in their struggle against the British colonialism of Palestine, then the Zionist-Israeli theft of it. The memories and testimonies of Palestinian women were captured to document their struggles against the Zionist settler-colonial forces of the past century (Abdulhadi, 2006a, 2006b, 2009). She eloquently asserted, "When we have our own narrative, with all details, then we can face the world with it."[27]

Moreover, shahadat and haki were also sources of data and methods of collecting more data. Haki, for example, may resemble an unstructured interview when it moves in the direction of a more give-and-take conversation. With time and spontaneity, trust is built, and even a structured interview turns into haki. Besides being a methodology, I argue again that haki is a tool of collecting data in an Arab context. In this sense, shahadat and haki are also tools to open spaces of reflection and sharing knowledge. Those who are practicing them or invited to act them all bear witness and learn from sharing intimate memories of oppression and ambiguities about daily personal and communal struggles.

Finally, I used shahadat and haki in this project simultaneously within a spiral process, not following a linear step-by-step or sequential plan. They became a hybridized methodology/method (Flores Carmona et al., 2018) approach in which shahadat and haki guided and depended on each other throughout the project.

Shahadat

The first methodology that drove this project is each shahada of three Egyptian women who experienced state-sanctioned violence. In Arabic, shahada is a public account of someone's truth

(Baheth, n.d.). Giving a shahada is a known mode of revealing truths in a formal legal setup. However, outside the courts, shahada is similar to testimonio as a spontaneous mode of telling truths to build up collective solidarity, especially as colonized peoples face militarist and imperial structures of violence and oppression. Co-constructing and building with Chicana epistemology, I used shahada as a "unique expression of the methodological as spoken accounts of oppression" (Reyes & Rodríguez, 2012, p. 256). Within a collective moment of struggle against oppression, a shahada is used not only to speak the truth, but rather to tell "an account from an individual point of view whose consciousness has led to an analysis of the experience as a shared component of oppression" (Reyes & Rodríguez, 2012, p. 528). My use of shahada in this study built on the Chicana feminista understanding that testimonios are tools of "breaking silences and bearing witness to both injustices and social change" (Delgado Bernal et al., 2012, p. 364).

The shahadat used here are Egyptian women's immediate public spoken accounts of oppression and their visceral experiences at an historic epic moment of Egypt's history. At the same time, I am using shahadat as a research Arabyya methodology that centers Egyptian women's experiences during suwret yanayer. I used shahadat as a methodology to validate "the lived experiences, and epistemologies of historically oppressed groups" (Flores Carmona, 2014, p. 118), in this case Egyptian women. This validation re-centers Egyptian women's 100-year-long positions and practices in the continuous revolutions of Egypt (El Said et al., 2015).

Egyptians, especially women, not only used shahadat to make sense of their bodily experiences in essuwra, but also as a political tool. Accordingly, they used their shahadat "as a means to bring about change through consciousness-raising" (Delgado Bernal et al., 2012, p. 364). They gave their shahadat on social media intentionally to expose the crimes of militarist and Islamist regimes, counter revolutionary forces, and their propaganda in the January Revolution. This way, shahadat can form a unique Arabyya methodology with a great potential to understand the central contributions of women to the revolutionary moment in Egypt through their embodied experience and their power in shaping and imagining a free and just Egypt.

Shahadat are different from oral history, storytelling, and other similar methodologies because they are intentional, political, and yet not extracted by a researcher or an outsider. They are direct accounts of the shaahedat themselves who are the creators of the knowledge. Thus, within Arabyya methodology, my responsibility in the research process is to mediate from Arabic to English. As such, shahadat are not only the data on which this project stands; they are also the methodology at the core of the translated narrative of Egyptian women's experiences in the Revolution.

Additionally, I borrow the Chicana feminista term "testimonialista" (Delgado Bernal et al., 2012), in Arabic shaahedat, to name those women who give testimonios. While this word is used to emphasize the power of women's knowledge (Latina Feminist Group, 2001), it is crucial to discuss the meaning of it in Arabic. The Arabic feminine noun "shaaheda"[28] is she who witnesses, she who is present and not absent, or she who is the knower and revealer. I am intentionally using the feminine term "shaaheda" for the women whose shahada are the center of this book. I used it also to encourage its use and to counter the dominant use of the masculine noun "shaahed," listed in major Arabic dictionaries on its own, erasing the feminine noun, which is rarely used, even in courts. Arguably, this absence linguistically conceals the shahadat of women and their importance in any context where Arabic is dominant. Not surprisingly, shaaheda is not used or asserted in the dictionaries when many Muslim-majority countries' women's legal testimonies are still worth half of that of a man. Interestingly, another form of this word, ashhaad, means the prophets and angels who testify about the deceivers and liars. Centering the use of the feminine term is specifically meant to counter the masculine dominant form, hence unmasking the linguistic absence of women from Arabic. This move of centering the feminine naming and excavating women's respect through language is a major principle of Arabyya epistemology/methodologies.

To me, shaaheda is the woman who reveals a shahada or reports what she witnesses of oppression. She is the messenger with free will who testifies and exposes the deceivers and liars. In this move, I intend to bring the value of the word and theorizing of Arab women to the collective everyday life, given its absence in any major Arabic dictionary and undervaluation in courts of Muslim-majority countries. This absence linguistically conceals the shahadat of women and their importance in any context where Arabic is dominant. Therefore, I am intentionally using the feminine term "shaahedat" to accentuate the women whose shahadat are the center of this book.

Haki

The second methodology guiding this study is haki. They are informal conversations or verbal, intimate, personal interactions between two or more people. In Arabic, haki is rooted in the verb haka, meaning to weave or tell (Baheth, n.d.). Haki is a daily practice of reweaving historical moments of dispossession to preserve the collective memory of Palestinians (Abdulhadi, 2017). It is part of a daily Palestinian practice of sumud[29] (Meari, 2014), a practice of perseverance, resistance and resilience, insistence to exit, or sheer existence in the face of the Israeli colonial-settler state. Haki is also an Arabyya methodology par excellence.

Using haki as a methodology in this study, I am again bridging with and building on Chicanas' praxis of pláticas to share knowledge through communication of thoughts, memories, ambiguities, and new interpretations (Fierros & Delgado Bernal,

2016). Then as pláticas, haki are the daily theorizing of oppressed people revealing connections between power systems, locally and globally. Haki is a methodology that colonized people use spontaneously to bear witness to and learn from shared experiences. They are intuitive approaches of conversing, storying, naming oppression, and making sense of one's life experiences with family members, friends, co-workers, neighbors, and so on.

Haki is an informal process of crafting the details of a hikaya[30] with which people make sense of their daily hard experiences. In collaboration with Chicana scholars in North America, I begin using haki in this book and call for its recognition as a way of knowing and a research methodology. Similarly, pláticas as a methodology has only recently been recognized as a feminista research approach, though they have been used for many years inside and outside academia (Fierros & Delgado Bernal, 2016).

Thus, the two Arabyya methodologies guiding this study are building on/with and speaking to Chicana methodologies as I am constantly crossing borders and living in translation between Arabic, English, and Spanish (Flores Carmona et al., 2018). Together, translated and bridged shahadat and haki enacted a transnational feminist methodology anchored in a politics of dissent and cross-border solidarities (Mohanty, 2013). Neither the shahadat or haki methodologies guiding this study have been formally used by Arabyya scholars, at least those studies trying to understand the experiences of people, especially women, in the Arab revolutions of 2011. Yet shahadat and haki are powerful methodologies that, I suggest, are urgently needed at this intense ultranationalist and hyper-patriarchal moment in Egypt and the world. They offer parallels between women's truth-telling and divulging of truth to power across borders (Flores Carmona et al., 2018).

Data Sources

Shahadat was the first data source that indirectly introduced me to the experiences of Egyptian women in suwret yanayer, before I had even officially begun the project. Haki was the second data source I deliberately used to learn directly from the three women who experienced the main tactics of state-sanctioned violence against women after suwret yanayer. The first prompt for this study was offered to me as suwret khamsah ou 'ishreen yanayer started and the Egyptians were (re)shaping themselves as the military took over on February 11, 2011.[31] Like Shereen Abouelnaga (2016), I clearly felt the warning signs when the military raped women detainees using so-called kushoof el'uzryyah a day after International Women's Day, March 9, 2011. By the end of November 2011, the shahadat of women such as Samira Ibrahim started to mount, unfolding evidence about kushoof el'uzryyah and the military's complicity with counter revolutionary forces.

In December 2011, I visited Cairo to learn about suwret yanayer firsthand, listen closely to those shahadat, and meet the women activists on the ground. However, a day after I left, images and videos of the public beating of a woman protester, "the girl in the blue bra," went viral. Having just talked to the protesters at the sit-in in front of the cabinet building where this incident happened, reading the public's responses, and seeing the massive protests of women, I spontaneously began looking for, attending, and collecting online shahadat of Egyptian women, especially those who experienced state-sanctioned sexual violence.

By the second anniversary of suwret yanayer, January 2013, there was a massive online flood of videos and text of Egyptian women's shahadat about mob rapes. It became clear to me that there was an urgency to understand and disseminate the shahadat of women in Egypt, those who were assaulted by the militarist and Islamist regimes taking over the Revolution. This move was the beginning of extending my scholarship to a more creative, transborder, translanguage, and political focus. Despite my geographical distance from Egypt, I felt a profound responsibility to try to learn, translate, and teach what was taking shape in Egypt by tracing women's bodily experiences with state-sanctioned sexual violence and their resistance within Egypt's revolutionary context. This is what Nagar describes as the ethical responsibility that requires both "*carrying* across and *retelling* … across time, space and struggle, while upholding a commitment to carry across meanings, textures, feelings and hauntings" (cited in Castro & Ergun, 2017, p. 124, emphasis in original).

The data sources used for this book are a result of an eight-year-long online search and five visits to Egypt. The data are focused on three particular shahadat as the most detailed, clearly articulated, and visualized accounts of embodied violations of women's bodies and the resistance of Egyptian women after suwret yanayer. The data generated and used in this study are also a result of a four-year collaboration (2015–2019) between myself, as an Arab feminist academic in the United States, and three Egyptian women, Samira, Yasmine, and Ola, all living in Egypt. I had extensive haki with each of them. These haki were both face to face and online through texts and audio. More of the shahadat were revealed in the haki with Samira, Yasmine, and Ola as we built relationships of trust between us over those few years. As such, haki became a tool to entice more shahadat, beyond what was already published online.

As a result of divulging more shahadat, a wider space was opening for more haki of trust. Flores Carmona et al. (2018) asserted that the buildup of trust in haki could also disclose additional testimonios or add details to previously shared ones. This is especially possible within relational spaces of vulnerabilities and pain. With more testimonios revealed, theorizing, analyzing, from the body becomes a significant outcome of the engagement between the researcher and the participant.

In the following, I will discuss the details of collecting and translating the shahadat and haki as online data and also through my research relationships with Samira, Yasmine, and Ola.

Online Data

Collecting the shahadat of Samira, Yasmine, and Ola began with my daily online follow-up of events in Egypt during January 25, 2011. At first, I casually followed prominent activists' tweets during el ttamntta'shar yaum [18 days] of the Revolution. However, my visit to Cairo in December 2011 led me to Facebook newsfeeds recommended by friends, activists, academics, and artists I met. On my last day in Cairo, a friend set up my Facebook account. With that, I began a daily, and more intense, search for sources and made serious attempts to contact Egyptian women making shahadat against state-sponsored gendered violence. I located several relevant online sources through Twitter and Facebook accounts of activists who were archiving and disseminating footage and comments about fast-unfolding events on the ground. By the end of 2011, the first public accounts of Egyptian women who experienced state-sanctioned violence were on my Facebook feed and the patterns and tactics of state-sanctioned violence against women were emerging. I closely reviewed and saved interviews with Samira, Yasmine, and Ola on non-state-owned Egyptian TV (mainly live) (Ahram Online, 2012; Akhbar El yom TV, 2012; EIPR, 2011; Ibrahim, 2011; Ibrahim, 2012b; Nazra for Feminist Studies, 2012; tahrirDiary, 2011b).

I reviewed hundreds of photos, graffiti, cartoons, articles, and civil society videos of, or relevant to, the three shaahedat who experienced the same state-sanctioned violence. I reviewed many shahadat about the context and the incidents themselves, and related lectures or public speaking events inside or outside Egypt available on YouTube. I have also saved screenshots of hundreds of related tweets and hashtags. I also reviewed and saved related press releases, reports, and documents of several Egyptian human rights, legal, and civil rights NGOs. I also reviewed documentaries about the women at and after suwret yanayer, including awassef al rabi' [*The Trials of Spring*][32]

(Levison & Reticker, 2015). The main online video sources between 2012 and 2015[33] were downloaded and saved in my files. All this related online material helped corroborate, substantiate details and chronology, and contextualize the shahadat of Samira, Yasmine, and Ola. Most of the material above was written in classical or colloquial Arabic and spoken Egyptian Arabic. I have translated them to English.

The core material for Samira's shahada included her postings on her blog, her Facebook account, and her statements on several online video recordings. I relied heavily on the first video capturing more or less a full account of Samira's shahada about her experience (tahrirDiary, 2011b). This was a video recorded at the end of November of 2011 by activists in the campaign of la lilmuhhakamat el'askaryah [No Military Trials to Civilians][34] (eight months after the incident). I also used the videos of the shahadat of two other women, Salwa Al Husseini Judah[35] and Rasha Ali Abdulrahman,[36] who went through the same experience as Samira (EIPR, 2011). Additionally, I relied on videos recorded later in February and March 2012 (EIPR, 2012a, 2012b, 2012c).

For Yasmine's shahada, I relied on her first live TV interview at the beginning of February 2013 and the documentary film alkhaitt wilhaitt [The Thread and the Wall] (Khaled, 2017). I used Ola's first live TV interview, which occurred the day following the incident, on the evening of Thursday December 6, 2012 (Foda, 2012), her video shahada to Mosireen[37] on December 13 (Mosireen Media Collective, 2012c), and her first online full shahada on December 11, 2012. I also drew on Ola's statements to the press after the court hearings in 2014–2015. I used independent media and civil society online sources as major sources for each of the shahadat.

Relational Data

The relational data of this study are based on hours of haki, intimate conversations with Samira, Yasmine, and Ola. The haki was the basis of building relationships of trust, reciprocity, and vulnerabilities (Fierros & Delgado Bernal, 2016) between us. Over a period of four years, I gradually built my relationships with Samira, Yasmine, and Ola. I shared my impressions about the event in Egypt and asked many questions to clarify the online data I had already reviewed. With Yasmine and Ola, we went over the details of their experiences to make sense together, both of us taking on the role of active researchers in this study (Flores Carmona et al., 2018). I also showed my interest in them as people, not only as "victims" of sexual violence. I gradually and genuinely showed my interest in getting to know them and building trust with them to start haki that reflected the aims of this study. The haki with the three women answered many of my questions on the online collected shahadat, and clarified their nuances and details. The haki helped me fill in the gaps or vagueness in their original shahadat. The haki with Samira, Yasmine, and Ola was the basis of the relational data of this feminist solidarity-centered study that built the trustworthiness of the final testimonial text.

Importantly, my relationships with Samira, Yasmine, and Ola were enabled by my older relationships with mutual friends and activists in the context of suwret yanayer. My dear friend, filmmaker, and artist, Nadia Kamel,[38] and some of her closest friends were key to the initial communication I had with Samira, Yasmine, and Ola. Additionally, as an Arab woman academic working in U.S. academia, still living in Arabic, I was not only able to read the spoken and written shahadat of Egyptian women, but also read them deeply enough to use them in timely and considerate ways as prompts to a respect-driven haki, and eventually a trusting relationship.

Samira

During my subsequent annual visits to Cairo from 2015 to 2018, I had the chance to meet Samira Ibrahim over tea or lunch in several public and private places. We met six times in Cairo, where we just talked and talked for a total of 10–12 hours. Sometimes she happened to be in Cairo doing some work away from her town, Sohag, while other times she made a six-hour-long overnight train ride specially to meet me. I have also been in constant communication with Samira using Facebook Messenger over trivial daily matters, including her activism in Sohag and her ambitions to continue her education formally and informally as well as study English. We also communicated over more serious issues, such as her participation in the parliamentary elections of 2015, campaigning as an independent candidate for the city of Sohag, and the assassination attempt on her life by the end of the campaign.

Though I spent a lot of time with Samira, she did not re-narrate her story about kushoof el'uzryyah and I have not asked her any related questions to what she went through in March 2011. When I first met her and introduced this research study, to which I invited her to be an active participant, she said:

> My shahada is all available online, you can get it there. I said what I needed to say. (Ibrahim, personal communication, April 16, 2015)

Additionally, to further illustrate the trust Samira had in me, early on she expressed to me more than once how several Western journalist and academics misrepresented her after a quick interview, especially in 2011 and 2012. She said:

> I wanted and needed to share what happened to me and expose the criminals. They wrote false information about me and about my family. They did not check with me before printing. They hurt me and hurt my case. They had an agenda and they did not really care about me and who I am. (Ibrahim, personal communication, April 16, 2015)

Yasmine

My initial contact with Yasmine El Baramawy was via text on Facebook Messenger. Then on October 19, 2015, we had an hour-long audio conversation on Skype. I only had the chance to introduce the study and listen to Yasmine presenting herself as a person. At this time, she agreed to participate in this study.

Almost two years later, I hosted Yasmine in my New Mexico home and we spent eight days together (October 23–30, 2017). I used this precious time to get to know her closely. I wanted to listen to whatever she was willing to share about what she had gone through since November 2012. This was when Yasmine trusted me with the deepest and most intimate details of the 90 minutes of the mob rape she had experienced, filling any of the gaps in what she presented to the public since the incident. We spent hours and hours talking about all sorts of matters and spending quality time together over food, yoga, a flamenco show, films, and more. Additionally, Yasmine shared her sha-hada with a group of close colleagues on campus. She played her oud, sharing a couple of pieces from her forthcoming album, one of which represented her resilience speaking with a painting of the Egyptian award-winning caricaturist Doaa Eladl,[39] abadan lan tuhzama rauhi [my soul will never break][40] (Eladl, 2017).

During this visit, Yasmine also expressed her interest in dis-seminating her shahada via an accessible and visual medium. This was a very special opportunity for me to prompt her by ask-ing, "Imagine there is a camera hovering above you and tracing your steps that day. What would it record?" As a result, Yasmine gave a minute-by-minute recounting of her experience in November 2012. She described every visual, bodily, audio, and even olfactory detail of the 90-minute organized mob rape she went through. She continued to elaborate on pieces of her expe-rience over many hours of haki. She did not want to miss or let go of any detail. She wanted to share her shahada with me fully once and for all. Next I met Yasmine three times during my visit to Cairo in June 2018. Throughout the past two years, we have been in touch constantly across the distance between the United States and Egypt. In July 2019, I invited Yasmine to Jordan.

I had the chance to catch up and see her up-close as a musician. She performed in two small music concerts in Amman.

Ola

I began communicating with Ola Shahba on Facebook Messenger on July 11, 2016, but we were unable to meet via Skype. Ola expressed her interest in the study. Finally, we met at Sufi Cafe in Zamalek, Cairo, on July 24, 2017. In a couple of hours, Ola re-narrated her five-hour-long horrifying experience of detention, torture, and sexual assault in December 2012. The limited time I spent with Ola was enough to solidify her trust in me and to give me her consent to publish anything out of our conversation. Though her online shahada was detailed, she wanted to make sure I did not erase the fact the she was also sexually violated. She said:

> I want you to include this part, because it makes me very angry that it has been ignored, though I clearly stated it on my first live interview on TV the next day. (Shahba, personal communication, July 11, 2016)

Additionally, the three shaahedat in this book, Samira, Yasmine, and Ola, met with me one more time in Cairo at the end of June 2018. They confirmed their consent to publish their words in this book. Yasmine and Ola approved the English textual draft of their shahadat and their profiles represented in the following chapters. Though Samira answered very few of my unobtrusive questions related to the actual experience of kushoof el'uzryyah, she told me that she did not want to read or have me translate what I wrote. She said:

> Go ahead, I trust you. (Shahba, personal communication, July 11, 2016)

This response from Samira emphasized that the act of feminist translation in this study was "not an empty space, a role that can be filled by just anybody, where truths are constructed through linear mapping of one set of ideas into those of another ... sharing via translation requires trust" (Hill Collins, 2017, p. xiii). With the three shaahedat, our communication and sharing was a "dialogical knowledge construction" via trust and within "epistemological border zones" (Hill Collins, 2017, p. xiv).

Thus, the relational data in this study were built over four years and over distance. They were built on hours and hours of haki and hundreds of text messages going back and forth between myself and Samira, Yasmine, and Ola. They were also built on the haki about the difficult ways of living after suwret yanayer, such as the closure of freedom of speech and assembly, censorship and surveillance, and so on. They were built on a special kind of trust that began the deep analysis of their shahadat as they expressed throughout what their experiences meant at the moment of the assault and later. Hence, my analysis of their shahadat and the final testimonial text in the following chapters could not have been possible without the relationships of trust we built with each other and working dialogically online, as well as during the many hours we spent together in Cairo.

My Researcher Positionalities

Similar to many people in the world, and especially in the Arab world, following the Egyptian Revolution of January 25, I was moved. The "18 days" of the Egyptian Revolution of 2011 captured my whole Arab self. The images representing *my* people, the Arabic chants, and the people's demands all spoke to my heart and awakened my wishes for justice in the Arab world. Following the hourly unfolding events, mainly on Twitter, my vision of a more just life in the context I call(ed) home was recharged. The calls and acts of the revolutionaries in public squares brought me back to the homeland and to my language. As an academic, I was deeply immersed in an imaginative and emotional state that was shaking my docility of living the distance in exile for the past seven years in the heart of the U.S.

Empire. "I wanted to be in Egyptian squares, I wanted to be inside the revolutionary process and its vision, and I wanted to live a new Arabness and a new home" (an excerpt from my journal, January 15, 2012).

My *difference* in relation to the shaahedat drove the conceptualization of this project, the data collection, and the analysis process. That is, my layered positionalities, my social and political locations and identities, my political and historical knowledges, and my linguistic literacies all guided the project. As an Arab[41] feminist and intellectual/academic teaching in the U.S. academy, I started as an outsider learning from a distance. I was eager to keep myself engaged with a crucial moment that will certainly shift how we know women and gender in the Arab-majority world. I was also trying to listen to the silences in the margins.

My first language is Arabic, and I use it as an empowering tool. In this sense, I have an insider perspective to reading the events, not only because of my literacy in Arabic and the history and politics of Egypt, but also because of the Arabyya theoretical perspectives that I draw upon. It is also because I have a long familial-political history with Egypt that makes me organically *homed* in Egypt and its revolution. I was inside the events in Egypt as I felt them viscerally and on every level of my being—following the events online, visiting five times since December 2011, and staying in close contact with friends and family in Egypt. Additionally, my literacies of Arabic and Egyptian history and politics at every stage of the project allowed me to maintain my insider positionality.

At the same time, I am not fully an insider, but rather I am an in-betweener (Anzaldúa, 1999), because I have not and did not live essuwra by physically being present in Egypt. Also, I am not a professional translator or a scholar of translation studies—I am more of the everyday and spontaneous translator between Arabic and English. Using my linguistic skills between Arabic and English, I move between activist and intellectual spaces (Baker, 2013).

The process of moving between these positionalities, at different stages of the study and with different people, especially the shaahedat themselves, was shaped by the challenges I faced. Sometimes I was read as an insider, which helped the research process, and other times this hindered the process. Throughout, my multilayered positionalities worked hand in hand with my use of critical self-reflexivity with every interaction with the three shaahedat. That is, I stayed aware to address how my privilege, power, and difference shaped the process of research (Leavy & Harris, 2019). I had to stay mindful of how to maintain a shared agenda throughout the study with the shaahedat. This is a serious engagement indicating "the critical awareness of [researchers] about the precarity of the praxis of feminist translation" and its "epistemic and geopolitical limitedness" (Santaemilia, 2017, p. 28). It is also, as transnational feminist Richa Nagar describes, a dance in which all participants involved are active "in the processes of (re)shaping, revising, and refining the narratives that emerge" (cited in Castro & Ergun, 2017, p. 124).

Data Analysis

My analysis approach in this study was built on a multilayered process of feminist translation (Castro & Ergun, 2017) and a poststructural process of what Jackson and Mazzei (2013) describe as "thinking with theory." This analytic process constructed the testimonial text in the three shahadat chapters and the claims I make in the final chapter.

Translation as a method of analysis is central to the feminist praxis of this study. Given that all the data were in written Arabic and spoken Egyptian Arabic, I first transcribed the original online data, the shahadat, and the recorded relational data, the haki, with Samira, Yasmine, and Ola into handwritten Arabic script. I read and reread the resulting Arabic text. I drew each shahada's timeline layered on specific locations on the map of Cairo. At this point, I was thinking *with* the context of the moment, time and space, and the larger context of suwret yanayer. I stayed mindful that the shahadat I was translating were fragments of these Egyptian women's experiences. Such fragments made the work messier, and hence harder for me to engage with a praxis of radical vulnerability (Nagar, 2014), "a place of co-creating knowledge as a continuously unfolding politics without guarantees" (Nagar, cited in Castro & Ergun, 2017, p. 124).

To make a cohesive script, I also threaded a corresponding piece of each shahada with the timeline layered over the map of Cairo. As a result, I then decided which of the Arabic texts to translate into English. I took this step as an interlocutor (Delgado Bernal et al., 2012) making a reflexive judgment that would be most helpful in constructing a trustworthy testimonial text. In this threefold first layer of analysis, I translated the initial data sets from their visual, textual, and oral forms to their Arabic transcribed written form, and then into their new textual English form.

The translation was a complex, evolving process guided by a passion for justice and inspired by the spirit of resistance of Egyptian women. It was a process that called for my very intentional engagement with the possibilities, as well as the impossibilities, of the translations as an evolving practice of building trust with the narrators and holding onto the faith of the power of shahadat. I had to pay keen attention to both the shahadat and haki and their "subtle issues of connotation and meaning" (Flores Carmona, 2014, p. 117). I had to listen deeply for the meanings that came out of the hearts of Samira, Yasmine, and Ola. Such listening required my persistent critical self-reflexivity throughout to assure that the English wording was not "unjust or harmful" (Flores Carmona, 2014, p. 117) to the shaahedat themselves or to the language, Egyptian Arabic. Hence, this level of analysis was an extensive and complex spiral process that offered a closer relational and deeper contextual translation. Often I consulted my friends and relatives in Egypt to help me translate spoken Egyptian words or unpack a contextual issue.

Throughout the translation process, my knowledge of English and Arabic became "a filter to move from one language to another" (Delgado Bernal et al., 2012, p. 385), bridging the shahadat for an English-speaking public in the North (Trinidad Galván, 2014). I became a shaaheda myself, one who was bearing witness to the three shaahedat's truths (Flores Carmona, 2014). I was another "holder of knowledge" in this study, "disrupting traditional academic ideals of who might be considered a producer of knowledge" (Delgado Bernal et al., 2012, p. 385). As such, translation also became an act of solidarity with the women of suwret yanayer and a commitment to convey the affect in their experiences (Baker, 2016). This act of solidarity is a cathartic conduit conveying not only the meaning of women's experiences in suwret yanayer, but also the feeling of the experience, as well as the Revolution itself.

I used the translation process as an ethical feminist guide as well as a tool linking theory to practice. Translation was a site where I extended the shahadat and highlighted the agency of the shaahedat. Hence, I used it as "a tool for changing the world ... a space of resistance, and a means of reversing the symbolic order" (Baker, 2013, p. 25). The translation in this study was more than a literal word-for-word translation. It was "not a straightforward or linear journey across languages, concepts or contexts, it is a dance—a complex back and forth between, among and across multiply-located discursive sites-with our fixed origin and destinating" (Nagar, cited in Castro & Ergun, 2017, p. 124). It was also a deep and non-literary translation process of highlighting the new knowledge of the shaahedat, in turn "enabling ideas to travel" (Hill Collins, 2017, p. xii) and cross borders (Trinidad Galván, 2014). This is what Patricia Hill Collins (2017) calls intellectual activism, because she asserts that work is "both speaking the truth to power and speaking the truth to people" (p. xi).

Particularly, I think of translation in this study as a transnational feminist process because it relies upon an "intersectional and heterogenous model of cross-border meaning-making" (Castro & Ergun, 2017 p. 2). At the same time, my translation process and outcomes of this study fill an "epistemological gap" (Castro & Ergun, 2017, p. 3) by making Arab knowledges visible and undeterred. My translation process entailed an epistemological confrontation that, I hope, counters and disrupts hegemonic narratives about Arab women and Egyptian women in suwret yanayer.

Next, in the second layer of analysis, I reviewed the English textual forms of each shahada. I did not use coding or thematic analysis of conventional qualitative data analysis, but instead I used "plugging in" (Jackson & Mazzei, 2012). Plugging in is a poststructural approach to qualitative analysis to reveal the elasticity of meaning in the data, which involves "reading-the-data-while-thinking-the theory" (Jackson & Mazzei, 2012, p. 4). To Jackson and Mazzei (2013), "Plugging in to produce something new is a constant, continuous process of making and unmaking … It is the process of arranging, organizing, fitting together (p. 262).

For me, this process of plugging in was not a one-time procedure of reading data; it was rounds of thinking and rethinking of the data. That is, I was making sense of the data and creating new meanings by thinking and rethinking with specific feminist theoretical concepts (Jackson & Mazzei, 2012). To do the plugging in, I was engaging data *with* questions of power, violence, gender, resistance, colonialism, militarism and Islamism, privilege, mediation, translation, and representation. I was also thinking *with* the main principles of the guiding methodologies of this study that allowed for a more in-depth theorizing of the shahadat power, hence forefronting the representations of Egyptian women's truths in an English publication.

Importantly, my process of thinking and rethinking with theory was simultaneously interwoven with the shaahedat's own continuous sense-making that they shared with me through every round of haki the past four years. At the late stages of the project and with my presence in Cairo, the haki turned into critical reflections that helped us build deeper understandings together and helped to create a common consciousness of the shaahedat's experiences (Flores Carmona et al., 2018). This form of analytical haki was part of a "reciprocal process" of analysis we could not have engaged without being "open and vulnerable" (Fierros & Delgado Bernal, 2016, p. 107) with each other. Hence, at this stage, the haki revealed fresh "personal theoretical insights" (Reyes and Rodríguez, 2012, p. 525) about the oppressions and injustices they went through. It also built at least a subtle alliance, if not a strong solidarity, between us moving across different contexts and spaces. This alliance that does not stop at the end of this project, but continues beyond as we are committed to the remembering and disseminating of women's shahadat and asserting their contributions in/to suwret yanayer.

The end result of my translation, thinking through theory and multiple instances of reflexive haki to analyze the data, led to layered meaning-making and, I hope, a more sophisticated representation of the three shahadat. It shaped the testimonial texts in the following chapters, as well as my theoretical interpretations discussed in the final chapter.

State-Sanctioned Sexual Violence against Women in Egypt

Public violation of women's bodies, both sexually and physically, after suwret yanayer was not the first time the Egyptian authoritarian regime tried to violate women's bodies in order to deter them away from politics, and specifically attempt to scare them away from any dissent (Hafez, 2014). Sexual and physical violence against Egyptians was used systemically by Mubarak's regime since the 1990s (Amar, 2013). Sexual violence against women was one of the many tools of torture Mubarak police and qwat 'amn edawalah [state security forces][42] used against dissent, mainly in detention (El Said et al., 2015).

One of the first incidents documented by the Egyptian NGO markaz el nadeem lita'heel dhahaya al a'unf wa ata'theeb [El Nadeem Center for Rehabilitation of Victims of Violence and Torture][43] was that of Amal Farouk.[44] El Nadeem reported that in the mid-1990s, Amal Farouk was "repeatedly raped while in police custody. This tactic was used to get her to reveal the whereabouts of her husband" (Carr, 2014). Another earlier incident of sexual violence targeting women activists in public was witnessed at a demonstration on May 25, 2005. At the time, protestors were opposing a set of Mubarak-proposed constitutional amendments (Zaki & Abd Alhamid, 2014). This was a kefaya [enough][45] protest against which the state security police unleashed their plain-clothed thugs on journalist Nawal Ali[46] and raped her at the doorsteps of naqabet elmuhameen [Journalists Syndicate building][47] in Cairo. This day was dubbed as al 'arbi'a el aswad [Black Wednesday].[48] In Egyptian activists' minds, this incident was the beginning of the Mubarak regime's intentional and strategic attack on women's bodies to break popular opposition. Referring to Black Wednesday and the rape of Nawal Ali, not as the first sexual assault on protestors, but the first time it was captured on camera, Dr. Aida Seif al-Dawla,[49] a psychiatrist and founder of El Nadeem Center, said:

> It took place in public and in such an organized manner, leaving no doubt that it was planned and premeditated. And contrary to what the assault was meant to achieve, it was met by defiance from the women and their female relatives. At the time the police had crossed a line and miscalculated women's responses. (Carr, 2014)

According to Abouelnaga (2015), this incident was "so fierce and ugly, [it] declared the female body to be a site of [political] contest" (p. 39) and, I argue, this experience rendered her body violable in public. This was the moment it became apparent that women journalists and activists were facing "an obviously new batch of police-supported thugs: the sexual harassment squad" (Kamal, 2016, p. 15).

The first incidents of mass sexual assault emerged in downtown Cairo during Muslims' celebrations of both Eid al-Fitr and Eid al-Adha in 2006 and 2007. Bloggers and several feminist organizations began writing about these incidents, warning of a new emerging danger that eventually escalated right after the downfall of Mubarak's regime in 2011. Police organized and hired squads who targeted and gang raped women in the squares and streets (Kamal, 2016) during and after suwret yanayer of 2011, and especially in November 2012, January 2013, and June and July 2013. During an interview with Reem Maged,[50] Dr. Magda Adli[51] of El Nadeem stated clearly the aim of the state "is to humiliate a nation, a people, a group, a tribe. The shortest way to this goal is to insult and assault women's bodies" (Balba, 2013). Right after Mubarak was ousted on February 11, 2011, the remnant regime's military and state security forces shifted gears. Sexual violence against women in public not only continued, but was intensified. Though it was mainly practiced in different public or state-owned locations in Cairo, next to or inside buildings or entities that represented the regime in power, these assaults became more visible in one way or another.

Next I describe four major events that represent programmed attacks or tactics of state-sanctioned violence against women after suwret yanayer. All the events described here occurred in Cairo during the two years after suwret yanayer. The transitional regimes during this period, the militarist and Islamist, were well aware of the power of women's participation in the resistance movement. This was the period when the Revolution was still ongoing as the people were fighting the counter revolutionary forces.

The four state-sanctioned tactics of sexual violence against women were: (1) kushoof el'uzryyah [virginity inspections or virginity exposures]; (2) beating, dragging, stripping, and stomping; (3) organized mob rapes; and (4) detaining, beating, and sexually assaulting. Each one of these tactics was distinct. Each tactic was linked to an apparatus of power and to particular groups who implemented the sexual assaults. The groups included special military forces or military police, regular police or secret police, state-hired thugs, and Islamist militias. Both the militarist and the Islamist regimes were using state apparatuses inherited from the old Mubarak regime. Therefore, these tactics were ready to be used as they were entrenched practices of quwat al'amn elmarkazi [central security forces],[52] Antiriot Police, elshurtta el'askaryya [military police],[53] and the militias of gama'et al ikhwan al muslimeen. It is also important to note the resemblance between tactics used by the army and the Muslim Brotherhood given that both are "hierarchical, patriarchal, secretive organizations with values [logic and practices that] are completely antithetical to the values of the Revolution" (D'Isidoro, 2019).

In the following section, I describe in more detail how these state-sanctioned sexual violence tactics happened at four main events over the span of 22 months (March 2011–December 2012). The chronology and naming of the four events discussed below begin to contextualize the shahadat (re)presented in the following chapters.

Kushoof El'uzryyah in an Army Base

A day after International Women's Day was celebrated in midan etahrir, on March 9, 2011, both soldiers and thugs in plain clothes violently attacked protesters, dismantling their tent camp in the midan etahir central garden, where protestors had camped since January 28. The military had set up a temporary base on the grounds of elmat-haf elwattni [Museum of Egyptian Antiquities][54]—at the northern edge of midan etahrir—after the January 25, 2011 protests began (HRW, 2011). Military officers assaulted protestors, men and women. They physically beat, electroshocked [tasered], and handcuffed them. Some of the captured protestors were also tied/chained to the iron bars of the fence surrounding the Egyptian National Museum. Others were badly tortured inside elmat-haf building (HRW, 2011).

Initially, 20 female protestors were arrested by military officers. Three of the women who were journalists were released. Rasha Azab[55] (28 years old) of Al Fagr Weekly newspaper was one of them. The military ended up detaining 17 women protestors and 157 men (EIPR, 2011). After being detained in the nearby elmat-haf for over six hours, they were transported to a military base in Cairo and held in military custody for four days. During this time, female prison staff strip-searched the women. One male military doctor forced seven of the women to submit to kushoof el'uzryyah [vaginal inspection], or what Egyptian military spokespeople later termed fuhoossat el'uzryyah [virginity tests][56] (HRW, 2011). Most women who were subjected to this shared their shahadat about being coerced to kushoof el'uzryyah. The army spokesperson admitted that it happened as part of a required "medical" protocol, mainly to inspect the virginity of detained women under their custody.

Samira Ibrahim is the shaaheda whose experience represents this tactical state-sanctioned violence in Chapter 3.

Beating, Dragging, Stripping, and Stomping in the Senate Building

On December 16, 2011, close to midan etahrir across from elmugama' el'elmi [Egyptian Scientific Institute/Complex],[57] the world witnessed heavily geared anti-riot police beat and stomp a woman on the ground with their batons and boots. They dragged her by the hair and ripped off her cloak, head cover, and blouse, showing her blue bra. A video and photo of this scene went viral immediately on the Internet. Marking their respect to this woman, the revolutionaries named her sit el banat;[58] in Arabic, it means the best of all girls or "Lady of all Ladies" (Abouelnaga, 2015, p. 55). In English media outlets, she was named "the girl in the blue bra."

The attack on sit el banat was part of a surge of military police and anti-riot police into the entry area to the parliament, the senate and prime ministry, and the cabinet building to disperse protesters. They were ordered to dismantle a two-week-long sit-in, which was an extension of the revolutionaries' tent camp in nearby midan etahrir, as well as to handle the confrontation between protestors and the police that was also occurring in the nearby street of Mohammed Mahmoud. The protesters were demanding a civil state "not dominated by military or religious institutions" (Amar, 2013, p. 32). They were challenging the appointment of a Mubarak crony as prime minister and calling for early presidential elections to end the transitional military rule of SCAF. After Mubarak stepped down, Egypt went through a transitional period in which SCAF became the de facto authority, consolidating legislative and presidential powers, as well as increasing their control through severe repressive practices by the intelligence agencies and police (Said, 2011).

On December 17, military police and masked special forces continued beating, dragging, stripping, and stomping women in the same area (Mikhael, 2011). They beat and dragged nine women to the basement of the senate building. In this makeshift detention space, they sexually threatened and tortured the women (Shewy Media, 2011). In those two days, four were killed and hundreds of protestors were injured and detained. These violent incidents and the subsequent related legal cases were referred to as ahdath magles al wuzarah [the events of the Cabinet Council].[59]

Since 2015, I have had a close relationship with one shaaheda of this incident, who later on voluntarily withdrew from the project.[60] When I indirectly contacted another woman from the group of nine above, it was simply too late and she was not able to participate in this study. Therefore, I don't include the specific shahadat of any women who experienced this tactic of violence. Creating relational data in this study was crucial to the theoretical framing and the core methodology, hence including only their public shahadat without their direct input was not an ethical option.

Though sit el banat maintained her anonymity (Yousef, 2012),[61] several of the women beaten and detained on December

16 and 17, 2011, came out with detailed public accounts about their experiences that day, and they are available online and in documentaries.

Organized Mob Rapes in Elmilyauniyat[61]

At the end of November 2012, several mob rapes were reported around elmilyauniyat [million people marches] in the streets around midan etahrir. Such organized rapes increased exponentially around the time of the second-anniversary celebrations of suwret yanayer, on January 25, 2013. A group of 50–60 organized, ordinary-looking men would cordon one woman at a time away from her companions in or around protests. Then they would isolate the woman in a circle to beat and repeatedly mob rape her in many ways for over an hour (Mosireen Collective, 2012b).

Mob rapes accelerated and became very vivid at this time when people were still protesting in the streets, because it was clear that performance of the Muslim Brotherhood's regime did not match the values and main goals of the January 25 Revolution. It was also a moment when Mubarak's police state continued its repressive business as usual (Mosireen Collective, 2012a). On November 22, 2012, President Mohammed Morsi, the first elected president after suwret yanayer, suddenly issued a constitutional decree in an attempt to grant himself broad powers above the constitution and any court in Egypt (EIPR, 2016). Morsi and his Islamist base, gama'et al ikhwan al muslimeen and hizb alnoor alsalafi,[63] were impulsively trying to consolidate power after less than six months in office. He isolated the prosecutor-general to insulate his decisions from any legal challenges (EIPR, 2016). This sudden "grab of power" (Amar, 2013, p. 35) signaled that the newly elected president was not interested in protecting the citizens or the Revolution and its goals.

In response, on Friday November 23, millions of people took to the streets refusing Morsi's draconian decree (EIPR, 2016).

In this context, the regime unleashed mob rapes to counter the people's resistance, especially the strong participation of women in these protests.

Yasmine El Baramawy is the shaaheda whose experience represents this tactical state-sanctioned violence in Chapter 4.

Detaining, Beating, and Sexually Assaulting in Impromptu Captivities

From December 5 to December 9, 2012, Islamist militias of the Muslim Brotherhood and the Al Nour Salafi Party attacked, detained, tortured, and sexually violated protesters who were at a sit-in in front of the Al Itihhadyyah Presidential Palace,[64] in Heliopolis, an elite northeastern suburb of Cairo. As a result, ten people were killed and over 700 were injured (EIPR, 2016). The area near the Presidential Palace was turned into an impromptu captivity zone, which was controlled by Islamist militias but also seemingly supervised by the presidential guards, military police, and state security police. This incident at the Presidential Palace came to be called ahhdath al itihhadyyah, the events of Itihhadyyah, or the Battle of I'tihhadyyah (Amar, 2013).

Ola Shahba is the shaaheda whose experience represents this tactical state-sanctioned violence in Chapter 5.

In keeping with the Arabyya feminist methodologies of foregrounding marginalized truths, I was committed to learning directly from Egyptian women in suwret yanayer. The shaahedat in this project are Samira Ibrahim, Yasmine El Baramawy, and Ola Shahba. I have maintained a trust relationship with all three of them since April 2015. These young women still live in Egypt and their shahadat expose three tactics of state-sanctioned violence used against women after suwret yanayer.

2 | INTRODUCING THE THREE SHAAHEDAT: SAMIRA, YASMINE, AND OLA

In this chapter, I introduce the three shaahedat to readers of this book to provide additional context about each woman. These introductions use each woman's own words to provide background information about Samira, Yasmine, and Ola before the representation of their actual shahadat in the following chapters.

Samira Ibrahim: "My Revolution Is Practical and on the Ground."

When I first met Samira in maktabet diwan,[1] in Zamalek, Cairo, on April 16, 2015, she introduced herself to me and shared what the Revolution meant to her in the following words:

> I am who I am, I am Samira Ibrahim Mohammed, I am of the streets, I am the product of the streets [public spheres]. I was born in 1986 and I am from Sohag.[2] I am the eldest and I have two sisters and a brother. I have an undergraduate degree in commerce and economics from the University of Wadi Egdeed, Sohag.
>
> I work independently without any institutional support. I work on advancing the political literacy of women in my hometown Sohag in the Governate of Sohag. I work to advance women's participation in political life and help them to get to a place where they are independent and do not need others. I work on different fronts supporting women's multifaceted issues. For me, it is a political battle in which women must take their rights themselves, without any handouts from anyone.

My revolution is practical and on the ground. I want to fight it smartly outside prison because I want to get to my goals. When the Revolution started, I was 25 years old and I was a marketing manager at a privately owned company. I was also freelancing with media outlets, writing journalistic reports. Though I am 29 now, I am actually 60, I really mean it. What my generation lived and witnessed the past few years is what those in their seventies have not seen throughout their lives. I have aged in the past five years living a lot of pain and huge challenges.

On the first anniversary of Mubarak stepping down, almost a year after her experience with kushoof el'uzryyah, Samira introduced herself to Basem Yousef on TV (Yousef, 2012). She described herself as a person who was always curious, critical, and politicized, beginning when she was 15 years old. She was aware of the regime's brutal security grip and their oppression of Egyptians. She recalled how in 2002, the state security forces mildly interrogated her for writing a simple essay for a school exam in Sohag.

On the same show, Samira introduced herself, stating:

I was only 15, in high school (eleventh grade). I chose to write about the horrific deeds of Israel at the time and not about the environment, which was another topic given to us. In the essay, I critiqued Arab regimes' docility towards Israel committing another massacre in Gaza. The prompt for the essay stated that "Arab armies are blocking the Israeli massacre of Palestinians." So, I wrote, "Where are those armies ... I never saw an Arab leader responding to Israel. Palestinian organizations and other Arab countries were meeting at the League of Arab States, they were repeating themselves, not doing anything proving their helplessness. I thought Egypt was the leader of the Arabs and should be solving their problems."

The next day the security forces pulled me out from the exam room to be interrogated at the police station, which was very close to my school. The security forces were mocking me because I was young, trying to fool me with sweets and juice, asking me, "Who is dictating you these ideas, who pushed you to do this?" They were assuming that I was prompted by somebody or by my father because he is a politicized man. But what I wrote was spontaneous. My father at the time was in detention. He was battling several indictments [with the security state], as a result of his fikr Islami [Islamic thought/ political leanings]. He was targeted even though he was not a member of any Islamic [illegal] political party/group.

On the night of January 24 [2011], I took the train from Sohag to Cairo knowing something was building up and people were meeting in midan etahrir to protest police brutality on yaum eshurttah, January 25. Around 11 a.m., it was very quiet around the Square. I decided to stand by the naqabet elmuhameen. State security forces started to appear, checking why there were some people assembling in etahrir, and began arresting people randomly. A state security man said to me, "Why are you standing here?" I responded, "Sir, I just arrived from Sohag and I am waiting for a relative to pick me up." Slowly protestors were trickling from different street entrances leading to the square.

The numbers were increasing by the hour. Although, I was supposed to attend a human development course, I stayed in the streets around midan etahrir all day. State security forces were running after protestors and beating us. I said to a friend next to me, "Being part of a 100,000 group of people here is better than a few tens in Sohag." The next day, January 26, I was arrested. I was taken to El Gabal El Ahmar [Red Mountain].[3] I was released on January 27.

People were out demonstrating in the streets; those are the people and they are not politicians or members of political organizations. They are oppressed and have lived injustices for too long. They are filled with anger and their anger exploded. They wanted to grasp their rights with their own hands. The people were out not to break into the Ministry of Interior as

the mainstream media was circulating. The security forces of
the Ministry of Interior were the ones who attacked peaceful
protesters.

I participated with the people throughout this year. I met
mothers of martyrs and many other people, brothers of martyrs,
or wounded and disabled. I met a young girl and I told her to
back off away from the battle zone. She said, "When we bring
the rights of martyrs, I will get out of here [will not protest
anymore]." Others told me, "It is not time for pure politics, it is
time for a fight on the ground, we are in the Revolution now."
Young boys as young as 17 were telling me, "We want to die
here." I was standing next to them and I was not afraid. People
were fighting with their own hands because the politicians had
not done anything so far. So, they were obliged to fight for their
own rights in the streets. If those responsible for the killings in
the events of January were indicted and punished, we would not
be here [where we are] today.

Yasmine El Baramawy: "I Am an Oud Soloist. All I Want to Do Is Make Music."

My first conversation with Yasmine El Baramawy was an
audio Facebook Messenger call on October 19, 2015. She was
in Cairo and I was in Toronto. She introduced herself to me and
shared what the Revolution meant to her, speaking Arabeezi, a
mix of Arabic and English. She stated:

I am Yasmine and I am just a human being. I have a BA in
English and translation. I worked for three years in PR positions
before I decided to follow my passion and learn and work with
music. I am an oud soloist, an instrumentalist. All I want to do
is make music, not a specific genre. This is not a position many
women take. I see myself making musical tracks for films and
performing in solo concerts. I started learning music in 2007,
when I was 25 years old, and took intensive music lessons
weekly with several master teachers until the beginning of the
Revolution, that is for three years or so. In 2011, 2012, and

2013, I stopped doing music. In late 2013, I performed one concert and uploaded one track online. After the attack [the organized mob rape she experienced in November 23, 2012], I drifted away from music, then resumed a year and a half after. I am now working on an album, but balancing between my music and my activism focusing on women's rights.

I lived and was raised in Egypt within its social and religious patriarchal ideas. When I was younger, I took this as the default, but when I was 12–13 years old I began to ask and see there is something wrong. I began to read and search around me. I figured that there are more important things than social norms that control our lives and ways of being. I realized I needed to depend on my own mind.

My mom is a professor of chemistry working in agricultural research. She was always my model, urging me to do the good work that is not only governed by financial or individual gains. I have mainly lived with my mother; however, for a short time before and after the attack, I lived alone. I have a brother, four years older than me, and he is married with a kid.

I was born in Cairo in 1982, so since I was born I have not seen anyone ruling Egypt except Hosni Mubarak. For 29 years, I have lived in this country not seeing anything but dirty streets, chaos, and corruption. I have lived in this country in which private rights of individuals are not protected. I considered this as the norm. I thought this is how things will always be and I will not see it change. However, my first participation with any real political action was in 2010, when I signed a petition with aljam'yya alwattanyya liltaghyeer [National Organization for Change].[4] I met a group communicating with the youth and I was moved. However, the beginning of my real political engagement was with the start of suwret yanayer. I participated and I was interested, I was in the streets and I had some hope for change. When essuwra started, I was living in the heart of Cairo when suwret khamsah ou 'ishreen yanayer started. I began my political activism during the 18 days of essuwra,

hoping for a minimal change. I was imagining Egypt would
be like Belgium or Denmark, the streets will be clean, and
people will walk on sidewalks. Yes, my imagination went in that
direction.

I had never joined any demonstrations before. Once I went to
the square, I was really happy. A revolution is about hope, about
change. It's about being better. (Schifrin, 2016)

Ola Shahba: "I Was Only 30 Years Old When Essuwra Started."[5]

When I first met Ola Shahba online on July 11, 2016, we
could not have a long conversation given that the Internet ser-
vice in Egypt was unreliable. Instead, we exchanged a number
of texts in which we began introducing ourselves in relation to
suwret yanayer, discussing Ola's central contribution to this
study, and the possibility of meeting personally the next time I
visited Cairo, in the summer of 2017.

Ola Shahba self-identifies on her Twitter account as "socialist,
living to struggle and learn" (Shahba, personal communication,
n.d.). She stated that she has been an activist for years before the
suwret khamsah ou 'ishreen yanayer:

I was a member of the "Youth for Justice and Freedom
Movement," which represented all kinds of Egyptians around
the country, and hizb elttahalof elsha'bi elishtiraki [Socialist
Popular Alliance Party] (Mosireen Collective, 2012c).[6]

In 2010, I earned a graduate degree in Anthropology from the
School of African and Oriental Studies. While I was in London,
I was active as a member of the Socialist Workers Party. For
years before the January 25 Revolution, I was politically active
as one of the founders of tayyar altajdeed alishtiraki [Socialist
Renewal Stream][7] and part of the solidarity initiatives of
majmoo'at al'amal al'umali [Workers' Action Group].[8] I was
meeting factory workers in rural Egypt—masna' ttantta llkitan
[Ttantta Kitan Factory][9] and masna' alsuwais llghaz [Suez
Gas Factory].[10] I also contributed to the effort of distributing

blankets and pamphlets/newsletters to the workers at sit-ins. I was also documenting the struggles of Egyptian factory workers and exposing the neoliberal violent economic agenda of the Mubarak regime.

A few weeks before essuwra, I was protesting again with a few people against the regime for not protecting churches and not valuing the lives of Coptic Egyptians. Later I was also participating in Khaled Said's Facebook page campaign and working with all kinds of youth groups organizing. In response to Khaled Said's Facebook page campaign, 20 protests erupted against police brutality on January 25. Paradoxically, this is the official day celebrating the "Police." Conditions for suwret yanayer had been building up intensely for the past ten years. The final straw that helped ignite our mobilization was the explosion of the All Saints Church of Alexandria on New Year's Eve. We knew that 'amn edawalah of the Ministry of Interior planned it to distract us from the dire situation inside Egypt, mainly the anti-police torture movement that erupted with the torture and killing of Khaled Said. On January 3, 2011, I was out in the streets in Shubra, Cairo, protesting in solidarity with the Copts in Alexandria after the most recent explosions of a church.

During the 18 days of suwret khamsah ou 'ishreen yanayer, I was on the frontlines protecting midan etahrir and fighting the central security forces. I sort of realized I did not get affected by tear gas right away, so I could hold a position on the frontlines longer than others, for about 35 minutes. I was the only female there with my comrades who were called "hunters." Their role was to collect active tear gas canisters and throw them back to the police side. On the day of indignation/rage, Friday January 28, one of my friends, Ahmad Dumah, was injured, shot in the eye. So, I took over his position on the frontlines. It was the day the people defeated Mubarak's police and thugs and we forced them to withdraw. On February 2, the Camel's Battle, I was injured like many of the protesters. I fell in an area full of broken bricks. I lost all my toenails.

During the events of Mohammed Mahmoud I, November 2011, the protestors clashed with the police and security forces. I was there to help the wounded and organize groups of men and women protesters. I ended up with a head injury.

I stayed active in 2011 and 2012, before the incident [on December 5, 2012]. I spoke about my experiences in essuwra and its sustenance, at several venues in Egypt and abroad. That is when I became active as a member of hizb elttahalof elsha'bi elishtiraki. For example, I spoke in Berlin at the Rosa Luxemburg Foundation (Rosa Luxemburg Congress, 2012). I asked my European colleagues not look at our suwrah in an Orientalist way, not to erotize it by saying "waw." I invited them to work and think with us to do a deep analysis, to learn together about each other's specific context, and to expose the parallels and connections between local and global rebellious movements.

Many Egyptian women, such as Ola, Yasmine, and Samira, used shahadat as a powerful political strategy of resistance against the remnants of the "old" regimes, both militarist or Islamist, who used violence against women as an oppressive tool to counter the Revolution. These shahadat are publicly spoken, first-person accounts about oppression with deliberate political intentions (Reyes & Rodríguez, 2012). They are powerful and political accounts, coming from the flesh, that reflect the central role and impact of Egyptian women on Egypt's January 25 Revolution and afterwards. Samira, Yasmine, and Ola each made powerful shahada about their different experiences of sexual violence committed by state forces after suwret yanayer. Their shahadat illuminate how each woman lived the assault, sought justice, and continued to resist the complex patriarchal nexus of militarism and Islamism. The following chapters represent for readers Samira, Yasmine, and Ola's actual shahadat. The three shahadat of Samira, Yasmine, and Ola stand on their own and are intended to be read uninterrupted and on their own terms.

3 | SHAHADA BY SAMIRA IBRAHIM: MILITARY-SANCTIONED KUSHOOF EL'UZRYYAH

"No, no, I got these girls from a whorehouse." This was the first indictment the military manufactured about us.

A man with a military jacket tested me [inspected my vagina] with his hands for about five minutes. It felt it was a long time. I was in pain. This is one of their tactics to end the Revolution.

This was done to break us and humiliate us so that we do not ever again think of fighting for our rights or participating in protests or protest oppression and injustice.

On March 9, 2011, Samira Ibrahim and 174 other protestors were beaten, arrested, then detained in a military prison. On March 10, Samira and six other women protesters were coerced to kushoof el'uzryyah [virginity inspections] by a military doctor. Those were the first state-sanctioned assault techniques used on Egyptian women present in the public sphere of suwret yanayer. On March 12, after four days of detention, a military judge decided that the protesters were guilty of seven charges and sentenced them to one year in prison, pending the completion of investigations.

In the following chapter, I represent Samira Ibrahim's shahada about her experience of kushoof el'uzryyah, the military-sanctioned sexual assault against women protestors. This testimonial text representation is specifically about her experience of getting stripped naked, searched, and coerced into a vaginal violation or rape by a military doctor. It is also Samira's shahada about pursuing a legal battle in 2011 and 2012 against the military and the transitional governing body, elmagles ela'la lilqwat almusalaha (SCAF). It is my own weaving of Samira's shahadat shared publicly, in pieces and at different times, since she was released on March 12, 2011.

Arrested, Electroshocked, Dragged by the Hair: From Tahrir Square to the Egyptian Antiquities Museum

At 3:30 p.m. [March 9], for the first time after January 25, the military forces attacked the sit-in at midan etahrir. They wanted to break it and end the presence of protestors in etahrir— maintained since January 25. I was part of this sit-in in the middle of midan etahrir, which included many women. What happened on March 9 was very humiliating.

It started with a group of thugs attacking us while the military forces close by were watching. Then they got in and were yanking the sit-in tents in the square and arresting whoever was in the way. [The military had tanks parked around midan etahrir and they used live ammunition too.] (tahrirDiary, 2011a)

I was among 17 women arrested and tortured by the military forces on March 9, 2011 (EIPR, 2011). The military forces assaulted all these women using several torture techniques, beating them, whipping them, dragging them on the floor by their hair, and electroshocking [tasering] their legs and breasts. (tahrirDiary, 2011a)

Seven of the 17 were sexually assaulted. The military forced on them what they call "virginity tests." This was the first series of assaults against Egyptian women's bodies by the Supreme Council [SCAF] after suwret yanayer. (tahrirDiary, 2011b)

This happened a month after Mubarak stepped down while he was enjoying his life at a presidential palace in Sharm El Sheikh [a Red Sea resort area]. He was simply moved from Al Ourubah Palace in Cairo to Sharm. Nothing deeply changed in the regime. We were at the time demanding a new constitution and transparent tribunals for Mubarak and the rest of those who perpetuated the regime.

By the external entrance to the museum (HRW, 2011), a number of military officers attacked protestors, beat them, threw water on them, then electroshocked [tasered] them and called them all kinds of obscene and insulting names. Imagine, they were also spitting at us.

They were beating many of us, arresting and dragging women by the hair and/or head cover. They took us inside the museum (HRW, 2011). An officer that I did not know approached me [later Samira learned that he was General Said Aabbas]. He said, "Hello, Samira! I have been expecting you! Come say hello." As he extended his hand to shake mine, he electroshocked [tasered] my belly. Then another presentable officer approached and said to Aabbas, "These girls have been protesting in the square, but they seem respectable. I will take them home. If they participate in the protests again, you can go ahead and arrest them then." Aabbas refused and said, "No, no, I got these girls from a whorehouse." This was the first indictment the military manufactured about us.

They wanted us to regret that we participated in the January 25 Revolution and that we made a revolution [revolted]. That day, I knew that they were trying hard to kill and end the Revolution. This is one of their tactics to end the Revolution.

Detained, Interrogated, Beaten, and Strip-Searched at a Military Prison

By 9 p.m. [March 9], after the officers beat us girls badly and tore up our clothes, they handcuffed us and dragged us by the hair, then pushed us into a minibus. It was a very cold night. We were muddy because earlier they threw water on us and dragged us on dirty floors. Our clothes also had spots where they electroshocked [tasered] us. We were not just beaten; we were literally dragged while handcuffed. At that moment, I was thinking to myself "They arrested us around 3:30 p.m., they tortured us, next they will interrogate us and let us go home. What else could they do to us? They have done everything possible at the museum."

Then the military officers brought a group of women all dressed in black cloaks. They were coming out of the museum. One of the officers instructed them to mix among our group on the bus.

In the meantime, these women were insulting the army officers in the most vulgar manner/words.

After spending the rest of the night on the buses, we were taken to the S28 army prison. As soon as we entered, they lined us up by a wall. One officer said, "If any of you dares to speak, we will bury her under the sand here. Nobody can see you or hear you here. Nobody will find you."

They asked us to hand over our belongings. They had taken my purse already and emptied it. So, I handed my work and club ID cards, my mobile, a ring I had on my finger, and E£50 I had in my pocket. Then they placed a set of knives and glass bottles that look like Molotov bottles in front of us. They took pictures of us with those items to "prove" that they belonged to us. They wanted to "prove" that the boys are thugs and we, the girls, are both thugs and prostitutes. I was thinking to myself, "Sure, we are coming from prostitution houses [brothels] and carrying all these items on us." Then we [17 girls] were taken into one cell in another building with a courtyard.

Rasha Ali Abdulrahman, another woman detainee, added to Samira's shahada:

Very late that night [March 9], the military officers began interrogating the detainees for three hours or more. In their minds, the Revolution was over and the protestors got what they were demanding (i.e. Mubarak's stepping down). In their interrogation, they kept asking the detainees why they were insisting on protesting and maintaining a presence in midan etahrir. They were asking them about their current demands. (EIPR, 2011)

Samira continued:

Thursday March 10, around 9 or 10 a.m., they bused us to Huckstep army base. As soon as we walked into a building, I could not help but notice that on the wall behind us was a portrait of Mubarak still hung up. It looked pretty new, with parts of the wrapping still on it. So, I asked, "Excuse me, sir, what is his photo doing here?" The officer responded, "So what! This is not your business. You whore, daughter of so and so. We love him, and you don't, he is our president, not yours. You have no say in this." (tahrirDiary, 2011b)

Rasha added:

Around 11 a.m. [March 10], two officers opened the cell and walked us out to another part of the building. Four women prison guards, Aazza, Huda, and two others, were around helping out with the procedures throughout the day. They lined us all up in front of a large room with two open doors and a window. One officer said, "It is time to body search you. Who among you has sustained any injuries?" I said, "Sir, we are all covered in injuries. We have been beaten badly." At this moment, I was escorted to the big room by Madam Huda. I went in thinking she will pat my body, the way they do bodily inspection at airports. I was quiet, not objecting, not saying a word, anyway I was unable to speak. Young conscripted soldiers standing outside the room were watching through the window and the open door leading to the hallway. (EIPR, 2011)

Samira added:

Then she said, "Take off your clothes." So, I took off my jacket and said, "Here, inspect [pat my body]." But she responded, "No, no, take off all your clothes." So, I responded, "Excuse me, but first close the door and windows." She said, "No, this won't work." I responded again, "At least minimize the number of those soldiers watching." Then she gestured to Officer Ibrahim to come in. He immediately headed toward me, beat me, and electroshocked [tasered] me, while shouting, "You whore, you daughter of so and so ..." (tahrirDiary, 2011b)

Rasha Ali Abdulrahman, who was also in the room, confirmed Samira's shahada on how they were humiliated during the strip-search. Rasha said:

I objected and demanded the need for privacy and said, "This is not acceptable. Privacy should be respected even between women. This is an Islamic ethical norm." The director of the prison shouted back from a room across the hallway from the inspection room, "If you do not cooperate with Madam Aazza [another female officer], I will have a male officer inspect you." I was very angry, and they were treating us not like humans, but like animals.

At some point, Madam Aazza was taking her time inspecting one detainee's body. She was shaking every piece of clothing that this woman just took off. Like all of us, she stood fully naked. Then Aazza patted this woman's hair, presumably looking for sharp or forbidden items, and suddenly asked the director of the prison if she should take the hairpins out or not. All these procedures were taking a long time and were meant to humiliate us, coerce us to stand naked and be patted. (EIPR, 2011)

Salwa Al Husseini Judah, one of the first detainees with Samira to give her shahada, added:

The orders were made clear. We had to take off all our clothes. Another man with regular clothes was also present and the female guard had us stand in front of him while she inspected our bodies. We were fully naked. I had to take off all my clothes. It was against my will. Of course, at the door and outside the window, the conscripted soldiers and officers were still watching, laughing, pointing at me, and using their phones to film us. Later they wanted to use this as evidence of prostitution. (tahrirDiary, 2011a)

Samira confirmed:

That very moment, I wished to die. Some people get a heart attack, why don't I get a heart attack myself, now, and die like them. (tahrirDiary, 2011b)

Vaginal Violations at the Huckstep Army Base

Shocked and with tears running down her face, Samira said:

Around 4 p.m. [March 10], a couple of officers led us out of our cells to another building in Huckstep. Then they pushed all of us into a hallway. They asked us to group ourselves according to our "marital/virginity status." One officer said, "If you are a madam stand here, and if you are a miss stand here." Another officer said, "Your virginity will be tested one at a time. Let's make sure who of you is a prostitute and who is not."

So, the 17 women gathered into two groups, unmarried and married. I gathered with the girls or unmarried women.[1] Then they started to take us one at a time.

The woman prison guard, Madam Huda, ordered me, "Lie down here, the bey [chief or in this case the doctor] will examine you." She stood by my head as I laid on the bed [half] naked. I asked the woman prison guard, "Please come from this side," hoping her body would cover my nakedness from all of those watching. But she refused. See how humiliating! They wanted to break us. At this point, I gave up and reluctantly opened my legs. A man with a military jacket [a lieutenant doctor named Ahmad Adel Mohamed El Mougy][2] tested me [inspected my vagina] with his hands for about five minutes. It felt it was a long time. I was in pain.

When he was done testing, he said, "You must sign here avowing you are a girl [virgin]," pointing to a piece of paper. So, I am lucky that I did not marry. If I was married, I would have been indicted in a prostitution case. They have no right to do this to us. However, in these circumstances, I was performing their orders.

In the paper he wanted me to sign, there were a few lines of text and a big gap before the signature line. The lieutenant doctor said to me, "Sign here." I said, "Excuse me, sir, but I will only sign right at the end of the text and not below this gap."

I refused to sign on an almost empty piece of paper. Over my dead body. I had a feeling if I sign at the bottom of the paper, they could insert more claims and accusations in the gap above. Any added indictments will get us into a bigger disaster. (tahrirDiary, 2011b)

Again, Rasha Ali Abdulrahman confirmed Samira's shahada about how military personal coerced them into a vaginal inspection. She said:

Officer Ibrahim was coordinating this inspection and said, "If any of you says she is a girl [virgin] and she is not, I will beat her up and fuck [rape] her too. Get it into your heads, the 'virginity inspection' is going to happen no matter what." Officer Ibrahim, Madam Aazza, another male officer, and another doctor were all present in the hallway witnessing the "virginity inspection." Every one of the seven unmarried women was asked to take off her pants and underwear and lie down on a basic steel medical bed and open her legs. The guy they called "the doctor" was young, perhaps 33 years old, tall with broad shoulders. He was first wearing civilian clothes, then as soon as the "inspections" started he put on a military uniform jacket. This doctor had a log sheet with all the detainees' names to check who was married and who was not. Once we were on the metal bed, Madame Aazza was reporting to the doctor the findings of the body inspection she had done earlier. She told him, "She has a minor khitan [female circumcision/genital cutting] and no other wounds or injuries." Then the doctor checked the presence or absence of the hymen. When he was done, he wrote a report and had everyone sign off on it. (EIPR, 2011)

Samira stated:

This was done to break us and humiliate us so that we never again think of fighting for our rights or participating in protests or protesting oppression and injustice.

Then after this assault and humiliation, the two groups of women were led back to the two cells. All night, officers were shouting, "You all have ruined the country. What do you want from this country?" They were pointing at the women and shouting over and over, "You are all whores and also thugs." They kept repeating, "You whores and sons of bitches, you have destroyed the country! What exactly do you want?" They were taking shifts beating us all night, four officers at a time. Officers continued to insult us with the most obscene words. They were taking turns as if they were in a competition. I was in shock to be tortured and humiliated by my country's military, specifically by the armed special forces [alssa'iqa]. They were practicing [special torture techniques] on our bodies. (tahrirDiary, 2011b)

Military Court Prosecuting Civilians: A Year in Prison and Seven Charges

Late at night, around 9 or 10 p.m. [March 10], after all this humiliation, all detainees were led to another building in the base. We were taken to sort of a courtroom, a big hall on the second floor in a building in Huckstep army base. We lined up in front of high-ranking officers. This was our first appearance as civilians in front of a military prosecutor. They brought their lawyers to supposedly defend us. They mainly asked us why we were still protesting in midan etahrir and as girls why weren't we staying at home. In their minds, the fact that we were present in the streets, public spaces, meant we were whores and midan etahrir was like Al Haram Street [a street with many nightclubs in Cairo, which some equate to a red-light district]. (EIPR, 2011)

The next day, Friday [March 11], we were taken to the big room with a military judge and some lawyers. It looked like a prepared theater, like a dramatic play. In this big room, there were some young boys, who were part of the case, lying on the floor, badly tortured, unable to say a word—they could not respond to their names when they were called by the prosecutor. They could hardly wave their hands. This scene did not move the judge at all.

The prosecutor recited out loud the charges they dealt us. First, attempting to assault military officers who were on duty. Second, possessing ten Molotov [explosive] bottles. Third, possessing blades, knives, etc. Fourth, breaking the curfew that starts at 2 a.m., even though I was arrested at 3.30 p.m. Fifth, obstructing traffic, while traffic was flowing freely that day and we were by the sidewalk, and not on the street. Sixth, breaking sidewalk brick. Mind you, the central security broke those during the 18 days and was throwing the pieces at us, the protestors. Finally, seventh, breaking parked cars in midan etahrir. If this is accurate, where are those car owners?

I said to the military prosecutor, "Sir, none of those indictments are true." He was supposed to defend me, but instead he began insulting me, and humiliated me more and signaled to an officer to electroshock [taser] me. I was not expecting this kind of position and behavior from a prosecutor-general. I was hoping he would be fighting for my rights. You see, when we were first told we are heading to meet the prosecutor, I said, "That is a mercy, I will face him and report to him the details of the assault," but I found him to be the same as those torturers.

Then the prosecutor said to me, waving a paper, "This is an order from the Supreme Council of the Armed Forces and the armed forces are accusing you of all this." I was shocked. I thought he was going to side with the truth and ease it on me. But instead, he was writing without listening to our shahadat. So, I denied all the charges, saying, "I have not done any of these accusations. How is it possible for me to be roaming in the streets carrying that many Molotov bottles or breaking the sidewalk brick? Everybody knows when and how it was broken."

Then the judge started reciting the seven charges against me. Then he stopped suddenly and asked an irrelevant question: "Since you are from Sohag, what brought you here [Tahrir Square, Cairo]?" So, I responded, "Sir, I work as marketing director at a private company which has a branch here in Cairo. I deny all those charges, sir." I wanted to be released. But he responded right away, "You have come to midan etahrir for a sit-in and you all look unpresentable [a mess]." At that moment, I thought it was my chance to explain why I looked so messy. I was expecting him to ask why I was in bad shape, all muddy with torn clothes. So, I started by saying, "The military officer did this to me …" Immediately, I was pulled away behind a line of military officers in the back of the room. I could not believe that the prosecutor and the judge were working against me. And the lawyers they brought were not capable and did not speak up.

Anyway, at the end of this charade that did not take more than 30 minutes, I learned that I was sentenced to a year in prison for seven charges pending the completion of a full investigation. Right then I decided to file a legal case against the military. I was simply afraid this will happen to other women. (tahrirDiary, 2011b)

Rasha confirmed Samira's shahada:

One of the girls reported to the prosecutor that the officers forced them to a virginity test. The prosecutor ridiculed her. As a result, she was immediately dragged to a side room for "interrogation." We were forced to squat down in a line facing a wall. We were then told, "If you turn around and look behind you, we will beat you up. Get it in your heads that the army is above everybody and it is a red line you don't overstep." Then all of us girls were beaten again and treated very badly. When one of the girls was asking about our release time because she wanted to call her family, an officer electroshocked [tasered] her badly. She had a heart condition and she almost died. They meant to scare all of us. (EIPR, 2011)

Home after Four Days of Disappearance

We were released the next day [March 12]. For four days, we were in military custody/prison/detention, with no communication with our families. As soon as the military bus dropped us in Ramses, downtown Cairo, I took public transportation directly to Sohag [a six-hour bus ride].

I walked into our home in Sohag. I did not say a word. They were sick with worry about me and were glad to see me alive. Gradually, I began telling my father what happened. At first, I did not tell him all the details because I was worried about his health. I was worried about him and not scared of him. I am very close to him. I respect him a lot and I am his friend. I told him that I was detained, tortured, beaten up, and was showing him the bruises on my body while I was crying. After a few days, I was able to tell him that I was among the women who were "inspected."

I told him that I stood in front of a military court. He responded, "History is repeating itself." He was not surprised; he expected this behavior from the armed forces. My father was also prosecuted by a military court for his political stands during the Mubarak regime. He also reminded me how the security forces of the Mubarak used to raid houses at night, terrorizing families of political activists. I told him that I was very hurt and sad because I did not expect this from them [the army]. Then he also reminded me that women protestors were attacked by Mubarak's regime's security forces in 2005. I realized then that the regime was again punishing those who resist it, the revolutionists, by assaulting their women in public.

Though my father encouraged me, it was my decision to pursue my rights in the courts. He assured me that he will fight with me through the courts. He said, "Remember, this is not only your personal fight, it is the society's at large."

Any time during the past few months when I felt discouraged, I drew on my father's bravery and continued my fight. I am determined to fight this legal battle until I get justice. I am sad and hurt because I did not expect such behavior from our army. We must stop this wrong. This is the only way to reclaim my rights. It is the right thing to do. (Ibrahim, 2011)

Pursuing a Legal Battle against the Military

Shortly after her release, Samira was the only one of the 17 women who filed balagh [a formal notification] about her experience while detained in the military base. She was seeking the protection of the law for being sexually assaulted and tortured. The first notification Samira filed to the military prosecutor-general, given that she was reporting about an incident that happened on a military base, was ordered and performed by military personnel.

With this step, and the media already reporting, military officials and spokespeople gave contradictory signals and statements about the "incident" of performing "virginity tests" on women protestors at Huckstep military base. On March 28, 2011, SCAF posted on the military's official Facebook page Statement #29 that the military authorities will look into the truth about the incident. On May 30, 2011, a SCAF general who was interviewed anonymously on CNN confirmed that kushoof el'uzryyah were conducted. Then again, a few days later, on June 6, 2011, a senior major general in the Egyptian army stated that the military cannot confirm or deny that kushoof el'uzryyah happened because the case is still "under investigation." Then, soon after, another contradictory statement was issued, "kushoof el'uzryyah should not happen again" (HRW, 2011). Such contradictions added to the mistrust of SCAF, especially because of the impartiality of the military prosecutor-general in such an investigation.

As a result, human rights lawyers from the markaz Hisham Mubarak lilqanoon [Hisham Mubarak Law Center],[3] the El Nadeem Center for the Rehabilitation of Victims of Torture and Violence, and the almubadarah almassryya lilhuqooq elshakhsyeh [Egyptian Initiative for Personal Rights (EIPR)][4] filed another legal case on behalf of Samira. The case was submitted on June 23, 2011, to the State Council. They submitted the case to Egypt's State Council, the highest common or administrative court to challenge the military courts and practices.

Samira indicted every military personnel who assaulted her on March 9, 2011, in the midan etahrir area and the following three days in Huckstep military base. She indicted those who ordered or carried out kushoof el'uzryyah as an act done under threat by a military person, and in this case a conscript military doctor. That is, Samira challenged the administration of the military prisons who ordered the doctor to conduct kushoof el'uzryyah in a military prison. Particularly, Samira indicted Ahmad Adel Mohamed El Mougy, a 27-year-old military doctor, for carrying out kushoof el'uzryyah procedures on her and the other six women from the total of 17 women detainees. She was calling for the punishment of the military personal for committing a "sexual exposure or assault/offense." According to her lawyer, Ahmad Hussam, Samira's persistent argument was that the "virginity inspections" were not done as a health exam, nor were they conducted in a private space. They were executed on temporary detainees as a sexual assault, a terrorizing tactic (Ibrahim, 2011).

Three days after Samira filed her case, on June 26, 2011, the deputy chief military prosecutor summoned her to take her shahada. Two weeks later, on July 10, 2011, the prosecutor summoned the military doctor on duty at the military prison, a serving member of the military. He denied that "the invasive procedure had taken place." Samira's lawyer, Ahmad Hussam, told Human Rights Watch that he was not allowed to attend that session. The Middle East Human Rights Watch's deputy director, Joe Stork, summed up what the military was doing with Samira's case, saying, "We can conclude that the generals, despite their promises, have no intention to investigate or prosecute anyone for this criminal sexual assault" (HRW, 2011).

Later, Samira commented:

As a result, I was given the runaround for months. I was waiting for a response from the military prosecutor. They kept delaying the acceptance of the case because the Supreme Council (SCAF) [de facto ruler of the country at the time] did not want to admit that kushoof el'uzryyah happened in a military base. This would automatically force them to admit that the army itself [they are] is the perpetrator. I had to pursue this case also because I, a civilian, was prosecuted by a military court and sentenced to one year in prison. (Ibrahim, 2011)

Insisting to indict military personnel, I began receiving death threats on my mobile with an unknown caller ID (HRW, 2011). Callers threatened me: "You better retrieve your report" or "This is going to cost you your life" or "Your end is the same as that of Khaled Said."[5] Then I stopped responding to any unidentified calls. However, every time I tried to file a report to the prosecutor-general about these threats, I would be told, "You cannot file a report because you do not have an identifiable number we can trace." (tahrirDiary, 2011b)

Months of Dismissal, Threats, and Silencing

On December 3, 2011, Samira filed the second legal case. She challenged the decision to refer her, a civilian, to a military court. With this, she challenged the charges of the military court handed to her on March 12, 2011, before her release from detention (HRW, 2011). She filed this case with the State Council, the highest common or administrative (non-military) court in Egypt:

I filed two major legal cases at the State Council. The focus of the first case was the indictment of every single person who assaulted me during the four days [March 9–12, 2011], from the director of the military prison, to the lieutenant doctor, to Officer Ibrahim who beat me and electroshocked [tasered] me (Ibrahim, 2012a). I filed the legal cases through the Egyptian Initiative for Personal Rights, the Hisham Mubarak Legal Center, the El Nadeem Center for Victims of Torture and Violence, Nazra for Feminist Studies, and the No to Military Trials campaign.

At this point, having been tortured and humiliated by the army, I realized that whatever they [the military regime and its legal apparatus] do from here on will not surprise me. So, I must persist no matter what. I knew that if I responded to the threats, dropped the charges, and stayed silent, what happened to me could happen to any girl in Egypt.

During this period, the lawyers, especially Mr. Ahmad Hussam of the Egyptian Initiative for Personal Rights, often helped me as a therapist. I was in bad emotional shape and was not confident about my decision filing a case. I was in pain. I called him at 2 or 3 a.m., not sure if I should pursue the case. I was still confused about my decision filing the case. (Ibrahim, 2011)

At the time of filing the first case, I decided not to share my shahada with the media. I wanted the case to take its course in the legal system first. However, after a few months of perpetual postponement of the official acceptance of the case, I was ready to share my shahada publicly.

With no response from the media or the military prosecutor-general, I stayed home for some time and did not participate in protests. Then in October and November of 2011, I began organizing with young people. I stayed active on the streets, organized and participated in demonstrations to keep people awake and supportive of the Revolution before it died. I was not afraid at all, but was worried that the Revolution was dying. Every day people were getting killed, revolutionaries disappeared every day, some got killed, some were detained, some were prosecuted by a military court and imprisoned, some disappeared. They were trying to annihilate the revolutionaries. They [the military regime] only want submissive people who say to them, "Long live the leader, long live the leader."

I called on the political parties of the time but received no support. They were busy at the time fighting for their piece of the pie, Egypt. I also began asking the media to help me out. Yet I was told bluntly by producers of mainstream media talk shows that SCAF's orders were clear about my case. They were not allowed to give me a forum. I was literally obstructed from offering my shahada on mainstream TV channels. Sometimes I would be ready for an appointment to appear on a channel that would get cancelled at the last minute because they received an order from the security forces forbidding them to allow me the airtime to repeat my shahada again. (tahrirDiary, 2011b)

In December 2011, five months since filing the legal cases, and after pursuing complicated procedures, the Supreme Military Tribunal stated that they were still looking into the case.

From Legal Erasure of the Military Indictment to Popular and Civil Society Support

Finally, on December 25, 2011, Samira was summoned to present her shahada on the first case indicting the military personnel. Samira's lawyer, Ahmad Hussam of the Egyptian Initiative for Personal Rights (EIPR, 2011), was not allowed to attend and deliberate the case. As a civilian lawyer, he did not have the status to stand in a military court, which is considered an exceptional judiciary in Egypt (Ibrahim, 2011).

A partial victory was celebrated on December 26 because Samira's lawyer was able to obtain a copy of the court decision banning kushoof el'uzryyah in Egyptian prisons. However, at the same time, the military prosecutor officially refused Samira's main charges of "vaginal violation," her rape. The charges were changed from a felony "sexual exposure or assault/offense" to "disgraceful/shameful act," hardly viewed by the law as mild misconduct.

On the same day, Reem Maged (Ibrahim, 2011) interviewed Samira and her lawyer. Though Samira's first shahada on November 15 (tahrirDiary, 2011b) was circulated via social media, this time she was able to speak up publicly on TV about what became popularly known as "the case of virginity inspections."

Samira spoke her truth against the powerful regime at the time, the armed forces, and their abuses:

I know they were exposing and violating our bodies with kushoof el'uzryyah to humiliate us. This clearly meant that they have the masculinist militarist mentality. They think they can break men before they even break women, and as a result they can break the whole society because exposing girls' bodies and assaulting their honor [raping women] is a tool they use in order to break the society and its men. It is a tool that is meant to humiliate us. Yes, many women were terrorized and were afraid to speak out. What persuaded me to speak up was that I did not want others to experience this, I did not want to see one more woman experience kushoof el'uzryyah.

Ahmad Hussam, Samira's lawyer, said to Reem Maged, "Samira's case calls for the punishment of the military personnel who ordered and executed a crime against Samira." According to the law, coercing somebody to a "virginity inspection" would be considered a felony, or more precisely a "sexual exposure or assault/offense" (Ibrahim, 2011). It is an assault done "under threat because it was executed by a military person, and in this case a conscript military doctor" (Ibrahim, 2011). Ahmad Hussam stressed that the armed forces undoubtedly commit-ted several crimes and assaults on women's bodies after the Revolution. Kushoof el'uzryyah are the first of many assaults against those women who are participating or have participated in the Revolution. Ahmad Hussam emphasized:

The armed forces have committed many crimes against the men and women of the Revolution. They are clearly using physical torture, exemplified in beating, stripping women of their headscarves and clothes, dragging them by their hair in the streets, electrically shocking the protestors and detainees, strip-searching detainees, videotaping women naked, and performing "virginity inspections" on women detainees in military prisons. (Ibrahim, 2011)

Samira added:

Given that I am indicting army personnel, of course, I had to file a case in their military courts. So far, it has been a charade, not a normal legal case. It is clearly a dramatic play. They [military persecutors] even changed the allegation from "honor assault" [rape/sexual assault] to a shameful act of "mildly offending one's dignity."

This interview with Reem Maged was less than two weeks after the famous incident of sit el banat on December 16, 2011, in which the armed forces stripped and dragged women in the streets during ahdath magles al wuzarah [the events of the Cabinet Council]. Samira and her lawyer emphasized to Reem Maged that the crimes of the armed forces against women have not stopped (Ibrahim, 2011). Samira said:

> You know, I was arrested at the events of magles al wuzarah on December 16, 2011, when many women were dragged in the street, stripped, arrested, and beaten. The military police started attacking the sit-in early in the morning. I was detained for two hours that afternoon in magles elshurah [the senate building]. As soon as they identified me, they released me. As far as I know, nobody reported going through the "virginity inspections" during detention. The military forces were concerned about getting reported again. (Ibrahim, 2011)

A day after the interview with Reem Maged, on December 27, 2011, the military announced its decision to prohibit "virginity tests" in all prisons. Samira considered these results of the struggle so far to be a victory for her and other women in Egypt. Later she stated:

> I know I gained one main thing [the major victory of this battle], the verdict of the state council which banned the use of "virginity tests" even in exceptional prisons. This means, from here on, if another girl gets arrested, it is forbidden to execute this on her. (Ibrahim, 2011)

On January 3, 2012, the military prosecutor officially changed the focus of the case from Samira's accusation of military personnel as perpetrators of a crime against her [a victim] to an incident of a "scandalous matter." This argument was based on the logic that exceptional courts, in this case a military court, do not accept cases from civilian victims and do not uphold any relevant law. As a result, they did not look into Samira's indictment of their personnel. However, they have oddly looked at the misconduct of the military doctor on duty, who Samira accused of coerced "virginity inspections." Hence, the military prosecutor instead indicted him for performing a "scandalous act" during military duty.

While this was another setback to Samira's case, a civilian judge ruled the humiliating practice of kushoof el'uzryyah illegal.

Persisting to Expose the Crimes of the Military

Since filing the case in June 2011, the Egyptian armed forces delayed the deliberation against Ahmed Adel Mohamed El Mougy, the military doctor who carried out kushoof el'uzryyah procedures on Samira Ibrahim and six other women in March 2011. The armed forces claimed that an investigation of the incident was underway; however, the actual hearings of witnesses in the cases did not start until the end of January 2012 (Ibrahim, 2012b).[6] The Supreme Military Tribunal held an exceptional session on January 29, 2011, and set the schedule of summoning the witnesses in the case. During the months of January and February 2012, the Supreme Military Tribunal conducted five sessions in which military judges heard witnesses from both sides (Ibrahim, 2012b). On February 6 they summoned the women detainees, on February 20 they summoned the director of the military prison, the doctor, and Samira, and on February 26 they summoned legal and civil rights activists. Again, Samira's lawyer was not allowed in, though the lawyers of those indicted were allowed to deliberate. Human rights experts and investigative reporters also presented to the court enough evidence to prove that the crime did take place and asked to reassign the case to a "truly independent and fair judiciary—not a body subordinate to the Ministry of Defense, itself implicated in the crime" (EIPR, 2012c; Nazra for Feminist Studies, 2012).

During this stage of the case, Samira had to go through an extensive process of presenting evidence. Women's, human rights, and civil society organizations diligently supported Samira and the case (Ibrahim, 2012b). Several testimonies of legal activists and human rights defenders circulated online, reporting the decisive conclusions of their investigations into the incident in addition to the clear human rights violation of the armed forces forcing civilians to stand in front of a military judge.

While the hearings were proceeding, contradictory statements were leaked from internal military sources about what happened in March 2011. By March 2012, international and local human rights organizations published their interviews with four members of the Supreme Council of the Armed Forces (SCAF). Carelessly, those SCAF members disclosed that "virginity inspections" were routine procedures necessary to prove the "un-virginity" of the women detained (Ibrahim, 2012b). Here, it is very important to note that General Abdul Fatah El Sisi, president of Egypt at the time of writing and the head of the military intelligence agency at the time of the incident, defended the "inspections." He stated that the procedure was necessary "to protect the girls from rape" and they were meant to "protect the army of possible accusations of rape" (Carr, 2014). That is, the "vaginal violation" procedure was used as a precautionary procedure to prevent women detainees from claiming they were raped under the army's custody, or in other words to prove women detainees' "un-virginity."

Straightforward yet conflicting statements were evidently more in support of Samira's shahada than the denying position of the armed forces that kushoof el'uzryyah took place under their watch and by their own doctors in March 2011. This contradictory logic was persistently used as an attempt to control the narrative about the incident of "virginity inspections." It was used to negate and silence Samira's shahada, but this attempt did not hold.

Samira is clear that El Mougy committed a felony and he is not innocent of the crime of sexual assault. Additionally, Samira stated that the military court did not take into consideration, deliberately or not, the fact that the inspections were not part of known health testing protocol, nor were they conducted in a private space according to medical codes. They were executed on temporary detainees, civilians, held in a military facility (tahrirDiary, 2011b).

Therefore, Samira continued to gain support from the people, activists/revolutionaries, and several human rights, legal, and women's groups, as well as civil society organizations. They intensified their pressure on several related public entities. For example, the same organizations through which Samira filed her case sent their position statement to the Minister of Health protesting the conduct of the doctor who performed the "vaginal inspections" on seven women in March 2011 (EIPR, 2012b; Nazra for Feminist Studies, 2012).

On March 16, 2012, the military court issued a final verdict acquitting both the administration of the military prisons who gave the orders and the military doctor, Ahmad Adel Mohamed El Mougy. The military prosecutor charged El Mougy with public indecency and disobeying military orders. Though this doctor was acquitted by the military court, Samira did not derail from her story that he coerced her into kushoof el'uzryyah.

Samira was interviewed several times after the acquittal of the doctor. She stated, with tears in her eyes:

> I see that I did not lose, I won and gained a great deal when the "virginity inspections" were officially banned [since December

25, 2011] and other girls won't have to endure them. In spite of the military's decision this time to exonerate themselves, I am still a winner. They are free to do what they want, this is their court and they won't get punished, because they are the judge and, at the same time, the opponent in this case.

I am in shock and did not expect the judiciary is that bad and would not advance justice. I thank God at the same time that they acquitted the military personnel responsible; it is a better verdict than giving them a light ruling. With this result, I will not proceed or pursue this case further in the military courts. My father advised me to stop my struggle through the military courts.

In relation to the court's deliberation that her shahada was contradictory, and that when she first encountered the doctor, El Mougy, in court, she did not identify him as the doctor who conducted the "virginity test," Samira responded:

The military's propaganda sent out more contradictory statements misquoting me. The truth is that since I first spoke out early on, my statements have been consistent. In the meantime, five military leaders already admitted to human rights organizations that the "virginity tests" did happen (HRW, 2011). However, due to their status, they did not attend the court session to testify. Additionally, I did not have a photo or a video to prove the assault. They can easily deny that the incident happened to me. Material evidence and the status of witnesses are important points to consider. (Ibrahim, 2012a)

From the Military Trials for Civilians to the African Commission on Human and Peoples' Rights

Immediately as the verdict was issued on March 16, 2012, protests erupted in front of the Supreme Court building in Cairo (Ahram Online, 2012). Coming out of the courtroom, Samira looked distraught. She was immediately received by a supportive crowd holding banners and chanting against SCAF and the military regime. At the doorsteps of the court, Samira stated that she was disappointed but not shocked by the verdict. All along, Samira was aware that it is impossible for the armed forces courts to convict itself or its personnel. She also stated on more than one occasion that the final verdict is clear proof of the corruption of the Egyptian military establishment and that their courts have let her and the women of Egypt down. At the same time, she stated that in a way, the verdict worked in her favor. Vowing to continue her fight, she said to a big group of supporters and reporters, "Now it is my right to resort to international law" (Hussein, 2012).

Six months later, on September 24, 2012, the Egyptian Initiative for Personal Rights (EIPR) and Interights, the international legal and human rights NGO, filed a case to the African Commission on Human and Peoples' Rights on behalf of Samira Ibrahim, Rasha Abdel-Rahman, and Jihane Mahmoud, three of the seven women who were forced to undergo a vaginal examination to determine their virginity. They were calling for a fair trial in civilian courts and clear prohibition of the procedure. Particularly, the case was filed against the Egyptian state, calling it to address "the failure of the Egyptian government to respond to violations by army personnel against female detainees, in what has come to be known as the 'virginity tests' incident" (EIPR, 2013a).

On behalf of Samira, Rasha, and Jihane, EIPR and Interights were also requesting that the Commission:

> advocate that Egypt prosecutes all perpetrators involved in this incident in civilian courts, as well as, reform the country's Code of Military Justice, so that incidents where the military are alleged to have abused civilians will be heard in a civilian court. (EIPR, 2013a)

Additionally, EIPR and Interights were seeking:

recognition that the forced genital examinations took place, and an undertaking that such examinations will not be repeated, as well as improved procedures in military prisons to ensure that those detained do not suffer violations of privacy and bodily integrity. (EIPR, 2012a)

Importantly, the case "alleges violations of the African Charter, to which Egypt is a signatory" (EIPR, 2012a). The African Commission accepted the case on December 3, 2013 (EIPR, 2013a).

4 | SHAHADA BY YASMINE EL BARAMAWY: STATE SECURITY-SANCTIONED MOB RAPES

Women of Egypt must oust Morsi, because this is the era of banal, senseless, and cowardly men. Those are men who suffocate their young daughters to teach them a lesson or assault and rape a woman in public to please the stupid and lusty bystanders. Women are braver than those men, and they possess tongues that speak the truth. I say this with all my respect to free men everywhere.

Hey, Muslim Brotherhood, your tactics of terrorizing the revolutionaries won't scare us and the slandering intended is your disgrace, not ours.

I wanted them to look me in the eye and see I am human, I am not a thing, I am not an object, and I am not only a body. I am in pain and in shock. I thought they must sympathize.

On Friday November 23, 2012, Yasmine El Baramawy experienced a harrowing mob rape in the peripheral streets adjacent to midan etahrir, Cairo. More than 60 men ceaselessly beat and raped Yasmine's body for 90 minutes. At the end of this long experience, a woman interrupted the assault and snatched away Yasmine, who was displayed naked on a car hood.

Mob rapes were intensely unleashed in the aftermath of the Revolution as another technique targeting women's bodies in public spaces in an attempt to terrorize and force them out of public spaces (El Baramawy, personal communication, November 23, 2012). What Yasmine experienced both during and after the mob rape was particular. These state-sanctioned assaults took place during the period in which protesters were still on the ground insisting on the goals of suwret yanayer, and they occurred under the watch of the short tenure of elected Muslim Brotherhood Islamist president Mohammed Morsi (June 2012–June 2013). These mob rapes happened during the ongoing eruptions of what was called elmilyauniyat [million people marches] after Morsi's draconian constitutional decree. Mainly, hired thugs and specially trained undercover state security forces initiated and orchestrated the rapes. The assaults also spontaneously picked up more momentum with the participation of men passersby.

Becoming an inevitable witness, the following is my own representation of Yasmine's shahada about her experience of a horrific 90-minute state security- and Islamist-organized mob rape on November 23, 2012, in Cairo. This testimonial text is about the rape experience itself, the silences of her close friends for two months after the incident, and her coming out with the shahada on live TV. It is my own construction of what Yasmine shared in public in 2012–2015 and with me in 2015–2018.

Ninety Minutes of Beating, Dragging, Slashing with Knives, Stripping, and Gang Raping

On Friday November 23, 2012, at 6.00 p.m., I was walking side by side with my girlfriend on Elqasr El'Ayyni Street getting close to the midan etahrir area. I love to be present in areas of clashes, but I do not participate; I usually stand in the back and chant. Those people who dive deep into the clashes are going to die; our presence adds to the numbers of people behind them as support.

Ten minutes later, as we got closer to etahrir midway before Esheikh Rihan Street, we stopped for a moment and turned toward sounds of chants and explosives. We were able to see clashes escalating between protestors and the security forces on the west side of where we were standing, around the area of Simon Bolivar Statue. Crowds were running toward us away from the clash area, running away from tear gas bombs.

I said, "Let's turn around and go back."

My friend said, "Yes, it is not a good idea to be in the area of violence/clashes."

At this very moment, a crowd was rushing toward us and getting closer. We were right on Elqasr El'Ayyni Street between Esheikh Rihan Street and Mohammed Mahmoud Street. As the crowd was approaching us, we both froze in our positions and put our hands up. Thinking the mob was part of the protestors, we both shouted, "Stay steady in your place, stay still."[1]

The mob, all men, rushed toward us and grabbed our bodies. For about 20 minutes, the men were forcefully groping our breasts and between our legs while reaching from behind. The men in the mob got to me and began ripping my clothes off. They also tried to rip my trousers off while touching me all over. I felt a cold breeze over my bare chest and realized I was topless. I was mainly on my feet standing and the men were holding my arms away from my body and trying to nail me to the ground while groping. My shirt and bra were ripped open but remained hanging on my shoulders. I was topless, but right away I pulled my red and black checkered neck scarf to cover my bare chest. Holding the scarf with one hand, I was pushing away the guys' arms with my other hand. My ID card and mobile were snatched out of my shirt's left pocket. This happened in a second.

Then suddenly a tear gas bomb landed next to my face and touched my chest on its way. For a split second, I felt I was floating on a cloud of gas. I could see white around me, imagining men's hands off my body. I was wishing to stay in this dreamy state. At this moment, all the men left my body and ran away, and I began to cough. A guy came to get me up. When I finally was able to stand on my feet, I held my friend, who was still close by after she was attacked, and we began running away from them toward midan etahrir. We thought it was safer to be among the protestors.

Now it is about 6.30 p.m. As we got closer to etahrir, the mob
of violent men returned back toward me. One of them targeted
the scarf and was trying to pull it off my chest. He knew I was
naked underneath it. He was pulling the scarf hard, but I was still
holding it strong and close to my chest. As soon as the rest of
them arrived, they outnumbered me. I found myself topless
again. I could see my friend and her friend Sherif running
toward me. They met in one spot close to me away from the
concentration of the mob. Sherif tried to pull me out of the
crowd. The men were choking and pulling him from his kufyyah
[black scarf]. My friend came close to me and was helping
me cover my naked upper body. At the same moment, several
men were pulling us away from each other. As a result of this
tugging, we both fell to the ground, my friend on top of me.
Then the men pulled my friend away while she was insisting
on not leaving me and I was trying to hold onto her with all my
strength. We were resisting hard. This is the point at which I felt
the violence began escalating.

This is when my friend shouted, "You are sons of dogs, you are
animals, you are …" I felt a surge of inspiration, so I shouted
back with more anger, "You sons of dogs …" We were both
trying to resist as we felt the violence intensify and take another
direction. They were proceeding to rape us. This was the first
and last time I insulted them with swear words. I immediately
got busy holding on to my trousers.

A that moment, I felt the groping between my crotch, over
my trousers. My trousers were still whole/not ripped yet. The
attack was intensifying on my body. I was now without any
help. I knew the mob was focused on ripping all my clothes
off in preparation for a more serious assault. My naked upper
body was exposed again. I was attacked by all 60 or more men
from all sides, groping all my body parts; hands were touching,
grabbing every spot of my body.

Now it is around 6.40 p.m. I was circled by more than 100
men. I was still topless. So, I realized that I had to hold on
to my trousers with all my force. With my left hand, I was

gripping the top end of my trousers. Simultaneously, many men were pulling my other hand to the other side. More than six hands were trying to rip my trousers off or pull them down. But my hand grip was strong. The trousers were getting ripped open from the back with knives.[2] That is when a hand suddenly went inside my trousers. Somebody forced his finger in my vagina. It was very violent. This was followed with more hands going inside me. While this was happening quickly, I was not screaming, but I was realizing that I am about to experience another level of sexual violence, that is getting raped. At that moment, I could not move myself one inch. I was overpowered.

The mob was glued to my body. As a result, I was dragged a few meters forward with every swing and pull. I ended up north on Elqasr El'Ayyni Street at the entrance of Mohammed Mahmoud Street. With the mob, I was suddenly pushed into a sewage water spot in the street. I was trying to squat in the accumulated sewage water puddle to avoid rape. The sewage spilled from the manhole, forming a visible 40 cm deep puddle. It was green and smelly. The sewage puddle level was a bit below my knees.

In this sewage puddle, the men in the circle were constantly trying to pull me up and turn my body around, but I was fighting back to get into a squatting position. I fought hard to stay in a seated position, albeit in the filthy sewage-filled puddle, because this was the only way I was able to protect my belly area. Though I found myself inside this disgusting hole, I realized that I can protect myself a little bit more in a seated position. This is the decision I had to take. It was a choice between standing up and being assaulted or sitting in a sewage hole.

So far, and at different moments of the attack, other young men were trying to rescue me by pulling me out of the circle. They would carry my body above their heads or shoulders and try to run. This was a position that put me in more danger because my body was even more exposed, and hence more accessible for sexual violation. Those young men could see the top area of the attack where the mob was violating my bare breasts but could not see the violations of my bottom.

Throughout, I have not stopped kicking with my legs and arms. So, I was actually mad at those men trying because while they were trying to rescue me, at the same time they were exposing me to more violence by those animals. They were also exposing me to bystanders who were happy to see me naked.

By 6.55 p.m., still moving as one mass with the mob, I ended up at an entrance of an alley branching from Mohammed Mahmoud Street. My body was filthy. It was covered with sewage, blood. Blood was dripping from my head, between my eyebrows. Then the mob ended with my body in a lit alley. It was suitable for those men watching and taking photos. One man shouted, "No photos, no photos" and put off the lit torch he was using.[3] I was thinking to myself, "No, no, take photos as evidence. Later I may be able to find online photos and videos of the incident that show my face clearly. I want to use them as evidence to prove the crime and restore my right."

Pulled and shoved again, we ended up at a small prayer place/ mosque, Masjed 'Ebad Elrahman. It is on the ground floor entrance area of a building with neon lights. This moment was very long.

I was getting raped and groped badly in a mosque. At one moment when I was on the ground with my torso in a seated position, a guy reached from behind and started to kiss my face. The moment he shoved his tongue in my mouth, I bit it very hard. He screamed out in pain. I was still holding my bare breasts, then the guy kicked my back so hard in response. At this moment, I was pushed and ended up on my back. A guy sat on my face while he was pinching every part of my body. I slipped my right hand between my body and his and found his balls. I squeezed with all my might. Note that my other hand was still holding my pants. It was crucial to note that when he moved off my body, I could see around me again.

Throughout this mob rape moment in the mosque, a few individual men were trying to get into the circle to rescue me, while the huge mob was attacking my body and very slowly moving in one mass from the entrance of the mosque to the exit side door. With the mob still glued to my body, we ended up in an area connected to the alley at the entrance of a building. I was placed standing with my back to the building's big iron door.

For the first time in the past 15 minutes or so, I was able to scan the view in front of me with 100 or 200 men around. I had a 180-degree panoramic view. I moved my eyes from right to left, where men stood at a three-meter high brick wall taking photos or videos with their mobiles (Khaled, 2017). Their huge smiling eyes and opened laughing mouths registered in my mind. This was the first time I saw faces. I wondered if those young men had any idea that I sort of caught them stealing a moment of watching pornography, behind their mothers' backs.

I was making eye contact with those men around, but they were all looking at my body and not into my eyes. I wanted them to look me in the eye and see I am human, I am not a thing, I am not an object, and I am not only a body. I am in pain and in shock. I thought they must sympathize. I did not see any life in their eyes.

Still with my back to the iron gate, I decided I am not moving until the door opens. I would be able to sneak in quickly and the door could be closed right away. I turned around and I could see the doorman through the keyhole. I asked him, "Open the door, do me a favor." I was begging him, but I was not even crying, and I have not cried up to this point. I had to get in and end all this. I heard the residents coming down the stairs, and heard them say, "We do not have the key." Right at that moment, someone put off the light inside the foyer of the building and the external entrance where I was facing the mob. I was in the dark again.

Now, as if we were in a washing machine, as one mass like a rolling ball, the mob and I moved again, a bit toward the sidewalk of this alley—between McDonald's and Hardee's fast-food restaurants. I fell over the delivery motorcycles parked by the sidewalk. I landed on a hot exhaust pipe. Given my body was fully exposed, parts of my skin were burnt. Then, as one massive ball, we ended close to a food cart selling hot fool [beans]. The owner reacted by directing at us the cooking gas bottle, spewing a big flame. It was so close to the left side of my face. I could feel the heat for a long time after this incident.

It is now around 7.10 p.m. I was on the ground again and the men were taking turns trying to rape me. I was still kicking with my legs and arms at the same time trying to protect my exposed [naked] body parts with my hands. But shortly after I stopped or slowed down [my resistance], the men would beat me more and callously whip me with belts, all over my body.

At this point, I was still on the floor of the alley flat on my belly. This was the most dangerous or confining position for me. I was unable to resist in this position.

From my perspective on the floor, I saw the tires of a car moving slowly toward my head. I could not move at all. The group of men close around me were pinning me to the ground. At the same time, they were fully raping me with their hands. I saw people's feet moving away from the car's route as its tires were getting closer to the left side of my face. I did not know if this car would stop or it was the end of me, my death. However, I was not afraid, and I thought to myself, "I must not give up. I may be able to save my life in this second before the car moves again right over my face."

An adrenaline rush gave me a boost of unexpected power. My hand let go of my trousers that I was up to this point still grabbing from the waist. Immediately, they pulled my trousers down to my knees. I did not care then, so I pushed up with both of my hands on the floor, trying to release my hair from under the tire or even cut it off. With this sudden rush of power, I was only able to turn my face to the right while I was still forcefully pinned to the floor. Suddenly, the car stopped 1 cm away from the left side of my head. My long hair was stuck under the tire and I felt it barely touch my head. As a result, and for a long time, unpredictably and involuntarily, my head would turn to the right.

With my hair still stuck under the car tire, and my head and upper body pinned to the floor, the men pulled my legs up. My head was snappishly twisted to the side, and they charged again to rape me. This was the moment they were able to get deep inside me. Unexpectedly and in a moment, the car reversed backward, letting go of my hair. As a result, we all fell backward. All in one ball. Then pulling me by one leg, they dragged me on the street. My back was getting badly cut. But I was still resisting, and I was able to lift my pants up and hold them tight again.

There was a lull of three seconds when I heard a bystander's voice saying loudly, "You are tough, girl." This voice encouraged me and suddenly gave me strength. But this opening or peace did not last. By then I was so tired and had lost my energy. I thought, "I should pretend to be dead, maybe they will let go of me." I was not resisting anymore, pretending to be dead. I actually heard people saying, "The girl died, the girl died!"

My body was floating in the air over men's shoulders. I imagined myself hitting Morsi. Then suddenly, I felt a sharp tool penetrating my anus area. It was extremely painful. I got another charge of energy and was kicking hard with my arms and legs, creating an opening around myself. Then I was on the floor, from the floating state to the yo-yo state. The mob surrounded me again.

All of this assault on the floor of the alley may have taken two slow minutes.

Then the men tried to push me inside a white car but could not. I was still resisting, kicking and jerking my body. Then four of them pinned me to the front hood. They were still violating my body in any way they could. I was naked [topless] but still holding on to the front of my trousers. At this point, somebody threw me a sheet from a building's balcony close by. I was happy and started screaming, "Cover me, cover me." But nobody did.

When I was pinned on the hood of the car, I was violated from every direction. This took a while as the car was having difficulty getting out of this very crowded alley. When the car moved from Mohammed Mahmood to Bab Ellouq, I was still pinned on the car hood by four guys. But I was holding my pants. We were moving into streets where there were hardly any people around. Close to Qasr Abdeen at the end of Tahrir Street, I saw Yasser, my friend, who was a doctor in midan etahrir, running after the car. Yasser was shouting, "Where are you taking her?" One of the attackers responded, "We are taking her to Abdeen to rape her fully."[4]

The car drove off for some time while the four guys were still pinning me to the front hood—from Bab Ellouq to Abdeen. Then they stopped or had to stop at a crowded residential area. I heard somebody say that we are in Abdeen. Perhaps now it was around 7.20 p.m.

The men were screaming, "Move away, move away, this woman has an explosive belt on her body." Right away, I saw a woman in her forties charging through and breaking the crowds in front of the car. She was wearing a black gallabyya [long thin cloak] and a bonnet. She said forcefully and loudly, "Show me the explosive belt, I want to see it." She threw a yellow milayyah [sheet] at me while I was still pinned down and unable to move away from the men on the hood. As the woman was shouting, "Where is the bomb? Where is the bomb? Show me!" she threw her body on mine to cover me. She was able to snatch me off the hood and pull me away from the mob. I stood still in front of the car with my back all uncovered—I was half naked. So, it was a difficult moment—I did not want to be seen naked. I kept holding my pants while covering my front body with the milayyah.

At this same moment, a group of men waving big sticks followed, clearing the space around the car hood. I think her husband brought help when he was at the neighborhood cafe. Then they quickly opened a pathway toward an empty shop nearby. As soon as we were at the door, the owner pulled down the shutters. But the woman insisted and began screaming,

"Open the way, open the way." We quickly went in and the shop's shutter immediately closed down behind us. Finally, I was inside this shop alone with the woman and her husband. The place was a small construction scene with bricks and cement. As they were shutting the door down, I saw Yasser arriving in front of the shop's door. We were inside, but the mob was still demanding to recapture me and was banging on the door of the shop shouting, "She is my sister, I want her out."

The three of us were facing each other. I was still wrapping my bare chest with my arms and my naked back was toward the wall. The woman gave me a gallabyya. But I could not let go of my arms to put the gallabyya on because her husband stood right in front of me aggressively staring at my naked body. He assumed that given I was naked in the streets and I was seen by people, I automatically approved his gaze [gave him consent]. I looked back at his wife, hoping she gets it. She did not tell him to look away, but instead held the milayyah as a curtain to give me the privacy to put on the gallabyya. In this exchange, and for a short moment, I was bare naked, and her husband was still staring at me above the milayyah.

With arrogance, the husband asked me, "Why do they want you? What do they want from you? What did they do to you?" I responded calmly, "They did everything." I was calmly trying to narrate what happened to me, but the husband insisted on interrupting me, asking again, "Are you 'miss' or 'madame'?" I responded, "Why does it matter?"

All this time, the mob was at the door of the shop, still banging on the door wanting to retrieve me. At the same time, the neighborhood people guarding the door were pushing them away. I could hear the screams of the men outside. Then I saw that Yasser was still at the door too. So, I pointed at him and said, "I know this guy, let him in, let him in."

They let Yasser in. As he approached and looked at me, he started to turn around to leave. I realized that he did not recognize me. I shouted, "Yasser, Yasser, it is me, Yasmine."

Yasser began crying, "I am so sorry, forgive me, please." Then he hugged me and whispered in my ear, "Where is Laila?" I said, "I feel Laila is safe." He responded, "I will go now to check where she is and let those people take you to your friend's house in Bab Ellouq." Yasser left. The woman and her husband asked me, "Is he your brother?" I said, "Yes." I did not want them to think I am a whore.

Then the woman was able to create a safe corridor toward her building to accompany me to her flat. We were going up the stairs and I could hear the mob was still outside the entrance, banging on the door and shouting.

Once we were in her apartment, she kindly welcomed me in. My body was covered with sewage and dirt, but the woman insisted on sitting me on her nice clean couch.

I asked, "What time is it? Where am I?"

The woman replied, "7.30."

In a second, the woman brought me a glass of juice and at the same time handed me an 8-month-old baby. I automatically responded and held it for some time.

The attackers were still waiting and banging on the building's door. The husband aggressively asked me again why the men at the door wanted me. The woman's sister and her very young daughters were present too. The husband started shouting at them, "You are not allowed to go out to the streets from here on."

After about 30 minutes, it was time to take me home after they got word that there was a secure exit away from the crowd banging on the building's door. They took me down the stairs through a corridor between the buildings and the side street entrance leading to Tahrir Street—where the husband's brother's car was parked. Yasser met us there. He told me Laila was with Salma now. We had to walk a bit in the small neighborhood. Once we were in the car, I said, "Take me to Bab Ellouq." The husband and his brother were in the front of the car, and I with Yasser and the woman in the back seat. We drove from Abdeen to Bab Ellouq.

When we arrived at my friend's building, I recognized a similar big mob of violent men banging on the building entrance. I realized it is too dangerous to be dropped there.[5] So, I immediately said, "Turn around and go to Elqasr El'Ayyni."

As they were approaching my building in Elqasr El'Ayyni, the husband was bombarding me with questions, doubting my story and trying to test my credibility. He asked, "Where do you live? What is the name of this hospital? Is this really your house?" I had enough, and I shouted, "What do you think I have done to deserve this?"

We arrived in front of my building, so I said, "Here, here, I will get out." The husband said, "No, wait, we will come up with you." The three of us took the elevator to the eighth floor. I got my apartment key out of the pocket of my jean jacket, which was under the gallabyya. It was just there, and not even on a keychain. I said triumphantly, "I have the key." This was an unreal or a magical realism kind of moment.[6]

The elevator door opened and Zainah was waiting there. I think Yasser called her and told her I was on my way. She was crying. She hugged me. At that moment, the woman and her husband left.

As I walked into my apartment, I dropped the gallabyya and headed toward the bathroom. Zainah saw my naked, wounded, bloody, and dirty back and screamed, "What happened, what happened?" My shirt was hanging off my shoulder and the back of my trousers were ripped—I was hardly covered.

I went into the shower and I was washing off my body, which was covered with blood, sewage, dirt. This was not *my* blood only; it was the blood of those dogs, or humans, or were they both? (El Baramawy, personal communication, February 14, 2013)

Exposing State-Sponsored Sexualized Violence against Women: An Anonymous Shahada

I wanted to come out with my story to the public right away, exposing the phenomenon and the pervasiveness of sexualized assault on women in the public sphere. So, the day after the incident, I asked a friend, a very respected and well-viewed caricaturist/cartoonist/satirist [Mohamed Andeel] (Andeel, n.d.) to visit me. For hours, I narrated and re-narrated the story to him, asking him to represent the horror of this violence in a powerful drawing the next day or week. I said to him, "Now that you have heard my story, I want you to draw it in a caricature, as you always do, expose political and social crimes." Andeel responded, "OK, OK. I am so sorry, Yasmine, you went through all this."

For the next few days or one week, I was having friends over to tell and retell my story to all of them. On November 30, a week after the incident, I had about seven friends visit me; one of them was Harara.[7]

By day nine, on December 1, 2012, when I realized Andeel did not respond to my request, I decided to do it myself. I called my author friend, Mohamed Khair. I narrated my shahada as he took notes. I asked him to publish it as an anonymous shahada under the initial "Y." Early in the morning the next day, December 2, Khair posted my shahada on his Facebook page, titled "The Shahada of Group Rape Incident in Mohamed Mahmoud." (Ibrahim, personal communication, December 2, 2012)

The following is an exact translation of every word of Yasmine's first testimony, though at that time it was an unidentified one. Mohamed Khair wrote on his Facebook account:

I received a phone call from my friend "Y." I am keeping her identity anonymous (until she decides otherwise). She asked me to publicly clarify that whatever media sources call "harassment incidents," they are actually mob rapes. They happened or are still happening around midan etahrir and they are actually more serious than "harassment." Over the next few minutes, she narrated to me the disastrous, painful experience that she went through on Friday November 23, 2012, and she emphasized that many other girls out that day or afterwards as part of the

Million Peoples marches went through the same thing. Now I leave you with her shaaheda.

Around 6.00 p.m., I was with one of my women friends, participating in the Million Peoples march against the milyauniyyet la lili'elan edstouri [constitutional decree]. We were standing close to the intersection of Elqasr El'Ayyni Street and Esheikh Rihan Street when several tear gas bombs were shot by the security forces toward the protestors in the clashes area near Simon Bolivar's statue. I started running with my friend, but a group of men suddenly ran toward and began attacking us. We fell down and they started ripping off my clothes. We saw a friend from afar running toward us trying to help, but the attackers captured him, and two of them started fighting with him and pulling the scarf around his neck, trying to suffocate him. We were both trying to resist, but the hands of the attackers ripped my shirt, my bra was underneath. Their hands stole our wallets and everything that is in our pockets. Everything in our pockets, our mobiles, were on the floor, and so was the friend who tried to save us.

The mob fled as other groups were approaching us. We started to run away from everybody toward Abdeen, away from etahrir, but we found ourselves in a big group of attackers, at the entrance of Mohammed Mahmoud Street. I was separated from my friend and we lost each other. The mob was pushing me and I was resisting, but I couldn't differentiate who was trying to protect me and who was trying to rape me. In a few moments, my clothes were totally ripped off, among the crowd of attackers, who held every part of my body, without exception. Then one of them violently inserted his finger in my backside. I started screaming and trying to reach a wall that I could see on the other side. I could see young men standing up high stand watching me and laughing. I was getting away from the attackers, and I sat on the ground, which was covered with sewage, hoping to protect any part of my body. They pulled me and one of them tried to kiss me forcefully, so I bit his tongue, and immediately he kicked me hard on my back. With the intensity of the pushing and pulling, I found myself held up high by a few men. I was kicking in vain, then I was taken to a place with neon lights, maybe it was one of the commercial stores in the back area of Mohamed Mahmood Street. I was unable to tell if whoever brought me here was trying to protect me or rape me. In reality, they had already raped all my body parts with their hands. The push and pull started again, and they took me out to the street again. I fell to the ground at the same time a car was approaching me among the crowds. The car almost ran me over—its tire was on my hair, and I was pinned to the ground before the car reversed. Those in the car tried to push me in, but they were only able to put my head through the window because of the pulling of the rapists. This was the beginning of a kidnapping attempt.

Then they put me on the hood of the car. Four men pinned me on the hood while others were taking turns raping me. The car moved, trying to get out of the crowds who were watching. We passed by a closed door, then a small mosque. We stayed in this state, moving slowly while people approached the car, saying very strange things about me: "This girl has a strapped bomb around her waist!" They were dispersing the crowd, making sure they didn't come any closer, because they were trying to save me. Then I heard one saying, "We arrived, here we are in Abdeen!" I stayed in this situation until we did really arrive in Abdeen.

In Abdeen, suddenly a woman leading a group of men with knives approached. They were trying to free me from all those crowded around me. They wrapped me with milayyah, but I could not move my body for those who were still holding it, and finally the woman and those with her were able to grasp me and take me away to a small shop with a closed door. They were banging on the door, banging until the owners of the store responded at the end and opened the door for us. They let us in, and by that point I was able to don the gallabyya, but the mob was still demanding to recapture me. They were banging on the door of the shop, shouting, "She is my sister, I want her out."

The woman and her group opened up a pathway to her house and we went upstairs and got into her house. Her husband started asking me, "What did you do to them? What do they want from you?" I was calmly answering him, but in the end I lost it when he asked me, "Are you a miss or a madame?" The attackers were still waiting and banging on the downstairs door. In the end, we were able to get out through another alley to the women's husband's car. We went away, heading toward my house in Elmnyara. In the meantime, the husband kept asking me to name the places around my house to make sure that I was not lying, and he insisted on going up to the door of my apartment! A friend of mine opened the door, hugged me while crying, then he left. The end.

Breaking Her Silence: A Detailed 12-Minute Live TV Testimony

For two months after Yasmine was mob raped, and especially on the second anniversary of the Revolution, January 25, 2013, organized group sexual assaults against women on the streets increased exponentially (EIPR, 2013b). Yasmine made her decision to break her silence and give her full shahada on live TV shows. She said to me:

> With this reality, I kept busy calling tens of politicians, human rights activists, lawyers, feminists, writers, journalists, and artists, asking them to publicize my shahada. When I did not get a response from anyone, I began to think of a strategy to come out publicly with my shahada. I know it was a hard decision to make, but I must do it. Because this violence has to stop. Not another woman must be hurt. I wanted to break the barrier of silence and expose those who are responsible for organizing and executing this systemic sexualized violence against women.

> On January 31, 2013, Reem Maged of OnTV interviewed me. I said, this is an organized and systemic effort to deter women from participating in the revolution. They want to terrorize us out of the public sphere. The exponential surge in the number

of mob sexual assaults to tens and hundreds in a few days showed that it is beyond a social phenomenon. It is a politically organized scheme that is targeting women to expel them from the Revolution, pacify their role. It is a major tool to repress women revolutionaries and break them.

In the past decade, sexual harassment toward women in Egypt has been accepted as normal. Blaming the girl and rewarding the manly behavior of the perpetrator is the norm. I think what used to happen is that women were exposed to a few harassing words in the streets. Then it developed into a very abusive language against women. However, lately it has escalated to serious sexual assault and even the use of sharp weapons. For years, the silence about sexual harassment was maintained. It led to this crime's surge and proliferation.

The vicious cycle is clear. The assault happens, people and bystanders are silent watching, women are silenced and blamed and shamed, then the attacks get repeated, so they are normalized, and so on. The media has been complicit by not speaking up.

On February 1, 2013, I made my first public shahada live on one of the private satellite TV stations (Fahim, 2013). I had a few minutes to describe the full experience of the mob rape I had to endure on Friday November 23, 2012. As I was narrating the horror of this incident, I showed my torn blouse and pants on the air. When I was done with this interview, I went to my place and found it full of friends. I told my friends then that I feel I am strong, and I am not how those criminals [state-sponsored media] want to portray me. I am not a victim; I am not weak.

Between 2013 and 2015, I was invited to testify on several TV stations and to be part of numerous documentaries aired in Egypt and many other countries abroad. In June 2013, I was also interviewed on MBC (Ahsan Nas, 2013). All along, I was focusing not only on speaking out my truth and exposing the organized sexual assault on women in the public sphere

in Egypt. I kept repeating my message on several TV shows. I
wanted to make it clear that this violence against women was
state-sanctioned, well-orchestrated crime.

At a local TEDx event in November 2013 (El Baramawy, 2013),
I said, the Islamist are involved in this organized and systemic
violence against women in the public spheres, and specifically in
the Revolution and demonstrations. They refuse to admit it, and
thus they refuse to hold those who have enabled and made this
violence happen accountable.

By the way, I refused to meet the Brotherhood prime minister
when he called asking to meet me. I was not going to talk to
anyone complicit with the perpetrators and more worried about
their regime's image than about women's well-being.

On the fifth anniversary of suwret yanayer, I spoke with Nick
Schifrin of PBS, and said (Schifrin, 2016):

They attacked me, and they stripped me, and they raped me.
And I was beaten. It was really violent. It lasted for 70 minutes.
If it was 15 minutes, if it was 20 minutes, it was 30 minutes, I
was learning all that time. And it felt like I had the experience of
30 years or 40 years in this hour.

I didn't doubt for a moment that this is a coincidence. I believe
it is organized and it happened to many other women that day
and later.

I changed from defending to attacking. I had this feeling that
the people must know, and we can't be silent.

All along, I wanted to specifically emphasize that the Islamists
in the regime had a major role organizing this violence
targeting women in this period. They were betting on women's
fear of the "culture of shame," and hence their silence. This
violence against women is more intense and more organized
and intensified than during Mubarak's regime. A huge shift
happened after the Revolution. It is a major tactic to counter
the Revolution and the revolutionaries.

I changed from defending to attacking. I had this feeling that the people must know, and we can't be silent.

[Before she came on TV] When I told my father, he said, "No, don't go on TV." And he threatened me that he will deny I'm his daughter.

They said, "Your girl is a hero." And he became proud of me. (LAUGHTER)

Everybody avoids talking about this, but when I did it, it became sort of a power to change the culture. I felt the need to say, "I'm someone. I have a job and I have a life and I do many things, and I have a brain I use, I have opinions, I have many things. I'm not just a victim of that."

5 | SHAHADA BY OLA SHAHBA: ISLAMISTS-SANCTIONED SEXUAL ASSAULT

At that moment, I was not worried about what they would do to me being a woman, but I was more worried what they would do to Rami as a Christian.

One guy forced his finger in my bottom. This was at the beginning, when they still thought I was a boy.

I kept thinking to myself that I must stay conscious and I must not cry.

On December 5, 2012, Ola Shahba was first beaten, dragged by her hair, detained, deprived from proper medical attention, and sexually assaulted by the Islamist militias in a makeshift detention area outside Al Itihhadyyah Presidential Palace in Cairo. She was dragged from the frontlines of the confrontations, which were located between the protesters at a sit-in camp and the militias protecting the president and his palace.

By the end of November 2012, when Morsi declared his power grab measures, millions took to the street and camped for days in front of Al Itihhadyyah Presidential Palace. On December 5, Al Nour Islamist Party joined thousands of the Muslim Brotherhood militias of Morsi's party. This was the beginning of the clashes between civilian protesters and the Islamist militias by the walls of the Al Itihhadyyah area. More than 700 people were wounded and five were killed that day.

In the following chapter, I represent Ola Shahba's shahada about her experience of detention, torture, and sexual assault by Islamist militias under the watch of the presidential guards,

military police, and state security forces. It is also about her legal
court struggle against Morsi's regime and the militarist regime
of El Sisi.

Protesters Detained, Tortured, and Sexually Violated outside Al Itihhadyyah Presidential Palace

On that day, both sides were going back and forth at each
other (kr ou fr) near Al Itihhadyyah. The first hour, the militias
captured two protestors—beating them, they broke the bones
of one. They were attacking the protestors with live bullets and
tear gas bombs. The protestors were throwing back broken
bricks. Casualities were falling from both sides for hours. I was
at the frontlines of these intense clashes. I decided to head to Al
Itihhadyyah Presidential Palace to stand in solidarity with those
in the sit-in who have the right to assemble and protest.

A bit after midday, I learned that the Muslim Brotherhood and
Al Nour called their supporters to join and intensify the attack
on the protestors. At that point, with my comrade Rami,[1] we
began moving toward the area of intense clashes. There were
few protestors with us at the frontlines, and those who were
wounded continued the fight and could not afford to retreat for
medical help.

I had a construction site kind of helmet on my head with my
sweater's hood over it. I looked like a boy, or not so much like
a girl. Rami had a backpack on his back and was tagging a
few meters behind me. To head to the frontlines, we both first
went through a side street behind. Both the militias and the
protestors were holding pieces of tin barricade sheets to protect
themselves from stones thrown in both directions.

The fighting intensified at the frontlines and most of those there
began to quickly retreat. As a result, some of the tin barricade
panels were falling. As Rami moved to stop the last panel from
falling, I headed over to help him. At that moment, we became
more exposed and the Islamist militias were fast approaching
towards us. We quickly began retreating. Rami tripped by a tin
barricade sheet on the ground. I returned to help him up, but

he began screaming, "No, no you move back too." Quickly, one of the Islamist militias appeared around the barricade and grabbed Rami by his backpack. Rami fell again. I threw myself on top of the militia guy to untangle Rami but there were other guys now pulling me too. At that moment, I was not worried about what they would do to me being a woman, but I was more worried what they would do to Rami as a Christian. I was dragged in one direction and Rami in another, with several militiamen around each one of us.

The militia dragged me on the street. Several militias were choking me and beating me at the same time with a stick on my helmet. I was pulling myself down to the ground, resisting being dragged. From there on, the Islamists, Salafists, and Brotherhood detained me, beat me, and sexually assaulted me for almost 50 minutes. One guy forced his finger in my bottom. This was at the beginning, when they still thought I was a boy.

Once they pulled the helmet off, they realized I am a woman. So, one of the militias said, "Oh, she is a girl, she is a girl," but the beating continued. Another responded, "Have mercy, she is a woman, stop." A few others said, "No, go on, go on, we need to teach all of them a lesson." Another said, "She has caused injuries on our side, she deserves to be beaten." The beating and the sexual violence intensified. Their hands were forcefully touching the front of my body, grabbing my breast while continuing the beating.

I bit the hand of the man holding my breast. He quickly tried to pull it off, but my teeth were still gripping his hand until it bled. I was happy to stop the sexual assault for a very short second. I felt good, extremely good, having the power to stop this assault on my body and hurt him in return. Then this guy forcefully grabbed and twisted my wrist. I screamed, "Why are you doing this?" He said, "I'm looking for the tattooed cross on your wrist."

They kept dragging me into a crowded area, at the same time intensifying the sexual violence, grabbing my breast and trying to put their hands under my clothes. I began screaming, trying to squat closer to the ground and refusing to walk further. Then they began kicking me and stomping my body with their shoes while still beating my head. Another was slapping my face hard.

I was screaming, "Stop, stop, stop. I do not want anybody touching my body." The guy slapping my face said, "You are a liar, liar, liar, nobody is touching your body. You are lying to us."

While I was insisting on staying in my place on the ground and resisting being dragged, I felt I was forcefully pulled in another direction, toward a parked ambulance car. Then a guy pulled my head to see my face and was about to slap me when I heard another guy in the background saying, "Leave her, leave her, I know who she is." Then he addressed me, "Weren't you on TV during the 18 days and you spoke against Mubarak?" He paused, then said, "She is not fool,[2] she is a respectable person. I know her."

I could see through the door of the ambulance car parked nearby. I saw a guy and a paramedic next to a wounded man. I heard one say, "He is our guy and he was shot in the face." The ambulance driver was a member of the central security forces.

At this point, one guy was trying to get me into the ambulance, and said to its driver, "Get us out of here." But the driver responded, "Get her out of the car, we need to move this wounded man to the hospital. It is getting more dangerous here." Then this guy helping me said, "Please be patient." The driver shouted, "Keeping her in the ambulance will put her in more danger." The state security man nearby said, "I cannot get her out of here. There is no way to get you out until you convince them," pointing to the Islamist militias.

At that moment, a guy with a black suit stepped into the ambulance. Everybody stood up, clearly signaling that he was a high-ranking member of the Brotherhood. Later I learned his name, Dr. Alaa Hamza. He was refusing to give the permission to move the ambulance. At this moment, the ambulance was getting shaken by a mob protesting my presence inside the ambulance. They were screaming, "Get her out, we want her out."

The guy helping me whispered to me, "Try to pretend you are unconscious." I leaned with my upper body to the side with my eyes almost closed. Then he said to Dr. Alaa, "We have to get her out of here." Dr. Alaa responded, "No. I have talked to the president's consultant and he is refusing to let her go."

Then Dr. Alaa took my backpack and moved aside. I saw him wrapping a bottle with a plastic bag. Then he came closer to face me, so I immediately said to him, "Check my bag right here in front of my eyes."

In response, he started to curse me, "You so and so, the daughter of so and so."

Quickly, he opened my backpack and looked inside it while I looked too. My bag already contained a plastic sheet to sit on when needed, a medical mask, a small money purse with keys, and my ID card.

As he pretended to search the bag, he said, "Do you have a Molotov in your bag?"

I said loudly, "No."

He said, "Yes, you do have a Molotov here."

Then he pulled out my little purse and opened it, then pulled out my ID card and asked, "What is your name?"

I said, "Ola Shahba."

He responded, "So you are Muslim. Then why do you fight us?"

He paused, then asked again, "What's your party?" I said, "The Socialist Popular Alliance Party." He asked again, "Is that Hamdeen's party?"[3]

I responded, "No, not the Popular Current."

Then he said, "Anyway, you are all communists, sons of dogs. And what brought you here?"

I said, "To rescue the wounded."

At this moment, the guy helping me opened the ambulance door and shouted to the crowd around, "She was only trying to rescue the wounded." The crowd shouted back, "No, she has to get out and still be beaten."

Then Dr. Alaa said, "You so and so, you are a liar. You don't have any qualifications to aid the wounded. Do you have any university degrees, any evidence?"

I said, "I have a master's degree."

Then he forcefully shoved my body and said, "Really, where from, you spoilt brat!?" I said, "London."

After a moment, I said to Dr. Alaa, "Please hand me to the police."

He said, "You think it will be a gentler experience? No, they will shoot you."

I said, "I would prefer to be killed by the police rather than by the people, those same people who once demonstrated together against oppression and tyranny."

This was the end of the conversation with Dr. Alaa. He walked out of the ambulance. I was left inside the ambulance with one of the Islamist militia guarding me. I kept thinking to myself that I must stay conscious and I must not cry.

Still inside the ambulance, I could see the guy helping me trying to convince Dr. Alaa to let me go. He was asking him to allow the ambulance to leave. His gestures reflected his refusal, and suddenly I was pulled out of the ambulance and Dr. Alaa said, "She must be detained." So, the guy helping me, with another guy, walked me toward a military police booth. Already sustaining painful injuries all over my body, I had difficulty walking, so I was leaning on them heavily. My body was partly exposed because my jacket was torn right at the beginning when they captured me, badly beat me, and dragged me on the ground.

The guy helping me said, "Here, please put my jacket on your head and hide your face." Going through a corridor of crowds, the two guys were protecting me with their bodies as the mob was insisting on getting to me while reaching with their hands, beating me on the head. Then the guy helping me shouted to the mob, "Don't worry, we are just taking her to the military police booth to interrogate her." I think he was genuinely trying to protect my rights, but he could not release me until he made sure they had another female in custody.

We arrived at a central security police barrier, which opened up for us to pass through, and we finally entered the booth, into safety. Then an Islamist militiaman rudely said to me, "Sit down here and *do not* move."

Another one said, "Shall we tie her up?"

The guy helping me said, "No need to do that, just keep her in the booth." Then he said to me, "Keep your head covered. We don't want them to take photos of you."

At this point, my eye was swollen and blood was dripping from my head to my face. I could not see well, but I could recognize that the crowds behind the police barrier were directing their mobiles toward me high above the barriers and videotaping.

They were also shouting, "Why would you put yourself through this? Is it really worth it to reject shara' ellah?[4]" I was thinking then, "I do not get what consolidating all state powers into the president's hands and the military and destroying civil liberties have to do with shara' ellah or Islam."

I was detained in a military police booth for hours in the cold of a December night. Once in a while, one or two of the Islamist militias would approach me and insult me with filthy words or shove my body very violently. One asked, "Why are you here?" Another asked, "Why are you all fighting us?" Another insulted me, "You so and so."

All along, I responded, "I am here to rescue the wounded. I am a citizen like you." I was saying this because I was hoping to reach out to the conscience of a human being among this violent crowd who were detaining and torturing other human beings like them. I was telling myself, "I must continue trying to engage them in sensible conversation."

I spent most of the detention time in this booth. It was situated right in front of the walls of Al Itihhadyyah Presidential Palace where a large number of male protestors were detained, all sitting on the floor, handcuffed, with only their underwear on. I could see my comrade Rami among them.

Once in a while, one of the militias shouted at them, "Which embassy do you belong to?" Another shouted, "Make sure to check their belongings to trace the bank transfer number and see who is funding them."

Another shouted, "Three thousand, ten thousand dollars."

Another shouted, "Yes, they are bastards, you are right, they are funded by foreign agencies."

"Funded by foreign agencies to create chaos in the country" was one of the claims they were trying to fabricate and accuse protestors of, in order to justify their detentions. During the time I spent in this booth, I witnessed more and more male detainees getting crammed in this spot, interrogated, humiliated, beaten, and left in the cold half-naked.

Negotiations and Release

I was still in the military police booth with what was left of my shredded jacket pulled tight to keep me warm. My mobile phone was flashing. It was set on silent all along. I hid it under the collar of my jacket. I looked in and saw the caller ID showing my friend's name, Mona Seif. I clicked on the green button but hid the phone right away. At the same time, I leaned forward to look outside the booth door to check my surroundings and report my location to Mona.

I whispered, "Mona, I am in front of Al Itihhadyyah Presidential Palace in a military police booth. I can see a green minaret close by. Rami is here too." I hung up quickly.

Then the phone was flashing again. I got two calls from my friends, Marwa Farooq and Samya Jaheen. I responded discreetly and said, "Please try to reach Mohamed El Qassass."[5] Then I quickly hid the phone again.

Later I learned that Khaled Abdel Hameed and other friends were trying to negotiate my release with the Islamists. Additionally, Samya reported live on a TV show that I had my phone on me but was still detained.

After this moment, a young doctor from the Muslim Brotherhood squatted in front of me and said, "I am so and so, I am a Brotherhood member from brigade so and so."

Then he started searching for the source of the blood on my head and said to me, "I cannot deal with your wounds fully here, but I will try to clean them up at least."

He cleaned the cut on my head and poured some kind of liquid on it from a small bottle. Then he handed me a thick piece of cotton to press on the bleeding area and said, "See how good we are. We are helping you out and giving you more attention and time than the other detainees."

At this moment, the crowds behind the police cordon were still watching. They screamed, "Hey, doctor, why are you treating her wounds? Let her die. Let her go to hell."

Then the guy who was helping me all along leaned toward the young doctor and whispered in his ear, "Say that she will die if she is not moved to the hospital and that her wounds need to be stitched." However, the young doctor said, "I cannot. This reasoning won't make a difference. They won't let go of her."

Then the guy helping me started to make several phone calls. This was all happening while I was aware that more detainees were brought into the area in front of the booth and they were beaten up. During those long hours of detention, I also heard a mother screaming, "Let me in, let me in. He is my only son." A militia screamed, "Who the hell let her in?"

Almost every hour or so, the two doctors would come by to check on me. But at some point I think they realized I was able to contact the outside world, so the young doctor came in with another guy I had not seen before and said, "Do you have a mobile on you?"

First, I said, "No."

So, he responded, "Everybody is aware you have a phone. Just give it to me without a fuss or they will come and beat you up."

I handed him my phone. At this moment, I could see a state security officer standing in front of the booth. It was clear he was responsible for the police cordon. He was talking to the Islamist militias and helping exaggerate their narrative about the detainees. He said as he was pointing at me, "What would you like us to do with her? Are you going to bring in a lawyer, then we receive her along with the rest of the detainees, or would you like to arrest them here?"

The Islamist militia said, "Yes, they are funded by external agencies." The officer responded, "I am sure they have Molotovs on them."

Then one of the Islamist militias addressed me and the other detainees, "You deserve this treatment and more." And the officer followed by shouting at me, "You are a whore."

After hours of detention, a young man with a dark blue outfit came into the booth, leaned toward me, and whispered, "I am so and so, and I belong to the Muslim Brotherhood brigade so and so. You will be out of here, don't worry, we received many phone calls requesting your release." Later I learned that at this time, my friends and comrades, Khaled Sayyed, Khaled Abdel Hameed, Marwa Farooq, and Professor Rabab El-Mahdi, were making phone calls to get me released.

Right away, one of the Islamist militias guarding the booth jumped on top of the young man with the dark blue outfit and said, "No, she will not be released. Who is she to get out?"

Another opposing Islamist militia said, "She is one of our ghaneemah."[6]

Another responded, "She is not better than our martyrs and she has to be humiliated more."

And another said, "We still have all night to teach her a real lesson."

Then I saw the guy with the dark blue outfit standing on the side talking to the other militias quietly, then he walked away behind the police cordon, talking on his mobile. An hour passed, then another guy with a gray suit came by. He seemed like he had power. Later I learned that he was the chief media man of the Muslim Brotherhood, Freedom and Justice Party. He stood at the entrance of the booth and said to me, "Do you know who I am?"

I said, "No."

Then he said, "I am Ahmad Al Sibai'. Why are you claiming that I am the one detaining you?"

I responded, "I only reported where I am. I have no idea who you are."

Later I learned that at this very moment, Al Jazeera TV were broadcasting live, showing the detainees' area of Al Itihhadyyah Presidential Palace. The footage showed that Ahmad Al Sibai' was present and close to where I was. As a result, he was implicated in my detention and torture by proxy. I think this footage contributed to my timely release (Foda, 2012).

Then Al Sibai' said, "Where do you live?"

I said, "Street so and so, in Elmuhandiseen."

He said, "Where exactly?"

I said, "At the intersection of Ghuzlan and Isam Hasheesh."

Another man interjected and shouted over us, "You are a bitch. You will not be released."

But Al Sibai' said to me, "I will get you out, but you need to tell everybody that I made it happen."

Suddenly, Dr. Alaa reappeared. Al Sibai' took him aside and said to him, "We are getting a lot of phone calls asking for her release. They are personally accusing me of her detention." He was trying to convince him that I must be released. But Dr. Alaa was arguing that the mob wouldn't allow my release because they were convinced I had Molotovs. I gathered that if Al Sibai' tried to get me out, he would be beaten up.

Al Sibai' said to Dr. Alaa, "You have to secure my exit with her."

Dr. Alaa said firmly, "No, we won't."

At this moment, I saw the Islamist militias' violence against the male detainees intensify. One of them was beaten up and mocked because he was cold and covering himself with a cardboard banner.

When Al Sibai' tried to get me out of the booth, one of the guards prevented him. So, Al Sibai' said to him, "Who do you receive your orders from?" He pointed to a man called Mr. Ahmad who was standing in a crowd of men discussing my release. The negotiations and phone calls lasted for a while. Al Sibai' was on his phone again. Then he returned and tried to get me out. Two guys slapped me, and another tried to snatch me from Al Sibai' again. I held tight to the arm of Al Sibai', who was arguing, "She has to exit. We have orders from El Biltagi."[7]

The guy who pulled me said to Al Sibai', "Let El Biltagi go to hell. She won't be released. She is like the others here. She will stay here and will be beaten up here." Then he addressed the crowds and enticed them, saying, "Come on, shout out, 'She should not be released, she should stay here.'"

Then Al Sibai' said to me, "I am still working to confirm the approval of your release." My immediate response was, "While you do that, I will not leave your side."

The militia guards who were in charge of releasing the detainees gathered around Al Sibai'. He handed them his phone to talk to whoever was on the line. The guys said to Al Sibai', "We have captured her several times. Every time we release her, she comes back. So, make sure she does not come back again."

Then they added, "We are allowing you to take her because we trust you and trust the names you listed."

Then I was pulled out of the booth and walked with Al Sibai' through a thin pathway among the detainees. I handed the guy helping me all along his jacket. He said, "No, no, keep it over your head so they cannot take photos of you." Al Sibai' also asked me to cover my head. However, as we took a few steps into the pathway, hands were trying to grab me, and some pulled me by the hair.

I was finally out of the immediate area of Al Itihhadyyah Presidential Palace. Al Sibai' handed me to my comrades, Mohammed El Qassass, Abdulrahman Faris, Islam Luttfi, and Mohamad Aabas.

Al Sibai' said to my comrades, "Hand me my reward for releasing her." Then he looked at me and said, "Make sure to publicize that I am the one who did release you in the end."

My best friend, Safyyah Eldine, and her husband drove me to the hospital. When I showed up at the hospital, my face was completely bruised, my eyes were black and shut off. Immediately, a doctor showed up and stitched the cuts on my head. Then he fully checked me and issued a medical report. This was the first evidence citing all my injuries. Then we headed west toward Masr Elgideedah far away from the Al Itihhadyyah.

First Live TV Shahada

On the evening of Thursday December 6, 2012, Ola appeared live on Yusri Foda's OnTV show with messy hair, a fully shut and bruised left eye, and visible bruises on her face (Foda, 2012). With clarity, and for the first time, she narrated her shahada on how she was arrested, tortured, and detained by the militias of the Muslim Brotherhood and Al Nour Salafi Islamist Party at the Presidential Palace sit-ins. This shahada was less than 24 hours after she was released. Ola said:

Yes, I was beaten with a club, I was choked and sexually groped. They assaulted my body everywhere, including my breasts. As a result, I have several stitches in my head and bad bruises on the back of my neck, my leg, and face.

I never imagined that I would be sexually violated by those who are members of political Islam parties. I think they constructed me as a half-Muslim, so to speak, so beating me and violating me was legitimate in their minds (Mosireen Collective, 2012c).[8]

Too bad I worked for the election of Morsi. I want him to know that I regret it now, after this experience.

The Islamists were accusing us of implementing a foreign agenda and that we were paid to protest. I want them to know that this is not true. There is nobody willing to give their lives or get wounded for any amount of money.

I hold Morsi and his regime responsible for the bloodshed of the past two days, for our detention and torture. I consider him not only responsible for abuses done by his supporters and Islamist militias, but also by state security forces and the military police. As president, they are all under his authority.

During the long hours of detention, I was focused on keeping my brain alert on four issues: (1) I must hold onto the details of this experience to expose them; (2) I must stay conscious; (3) I must not cry; and (4) they must know that they cannot break my soul. I was also very aware that I am politically organized, and hence I will have the support from my party once they know what happened to me in this detention. In other words, I have more privilege and agency to use in this case, more than those who are marginalized or poor. (Shahba, personal communication, December 11, 2012).

Since she was released on December 6, 2012, Ola continued to expose the perpetrators of the violence that day at Al Itihhadyyah Presidential Palace. She used alternative online media sources, private and non-state TV, and the courts.

A Brave Shahada at Court

Ola filed charges against the members of Morsi's government and the Islamist parties involved, the Muslim Brotherhood and Al Nour. The charges included Dr. Alaa Hamza, the minister of interior Mahmood Ibrahim, leaders at the Muslim Brotherhood headquarters, Morsi himself, and the defense minister (present Egyptian president Abdel Fattah El Sisi). She accused them of assaulting her physically and sexually at the Al Itihhadyyah Presidential Palace events on December 5, 2012. Though Ola began the procedure to report the incident immediately in December 2012, the actual filing of the legal case was delayed until the beginning of January 2013. During this period, the prosecutor-general[9] was on strike, protesting that President Morsi demoted him to a position outside Cairo.

The larger case, known in the media as the incidents of Al Itihhadyyah, was postponed several times. However, when the final trials began, President Morsi was among the defendants. This case was filed at the criminal court of Cairo as case #10790/101 of 2013 (EIPR, 2016). The trial started on June 17, 2013, two weeks before the military ousted Morsi on July 3, 2013.[10] However, once Morsi was ousted by the military forces, more defendants were added, including Morsi himself and other high-ranking Muslim Brotherhood leaders. With this sudden shift of power in Egypt, the larger case of Al Itihhadyyah got more complicated and the prosecutor-general had to postpone activating the case to August 31, 2013 (EIPR, 2016).

At the criminal court of Cairo, Ola was finally able to give her shahada for the first time in person, on May 14, 2014. She said:

> The security forces are responsible for the violence [at the Al Itihhadyyah incident]. I asked a member of the police forces [standing next to me when I was detained by the walls of the Presidential Palace] to release me from the grip of the Muslim Brotherhood militia; he refused. He basically allowed them to physically beat me up (EIPR, 2016).

Originally, I submitted a report to the prosecutor-general indicting the minister of interior, the minister of defense, the Muslim Brotherhood executive office, and Nader Bakkar of El Nour Party, who called for and enticed violence against the protestors outside the palace walls, specifically by door #4. However, the prosecutor-general ignored my report. He focused the trial deliberation on whoever he wanted and excluded many others.

As a result of this round of litigation, the court charged Dr. Alaa Hamza for detaining and torturing the protesters. Hamza was the Muslim Brotherhood doctor who briefly attended Ola's wounds.

On April 21, 2015, the criminal court issued its verdict by acquitting Morsi and his assistants from killing protesters. This was clearly read as a politicized decision. It annulled the responsibility of the Islamist regime at the time, as well as the deep state of Mubarak. The annulation acquitted both regimes' representatives, from the police, the military forces, and the ministry of interior, to the presidential guard. To Ola, they were all partners in killing ten people that day. It was also an unjust decision because it erased the possibility of any kind of acknowledgment of the real crimes, and hence reparations for the victims of this incident. Ola commented on this verdict as a denial of the civil rights of many Egyptians, and therefore a denial of any reparations:

> I refuse this verdict in all its details, not only because it also acquitted all of those who participated, verbally or physically, violating my rights and tens of others, but I also refuse it because it violates the rights of those purposefully selected and referred to trial. It tries to assert the power of the court, but it is actually unjust and politicized, reflecting the power struggle between the current regime and Morsi's previous Islamist regime.

At the courthouse in front of the police academy in the district of New Cairo, Ola stood with her lawyer, Hoda Nasrallah from the Egyptian Initiative for Personal Rights (EIPR). Nasrallah highlighted that Ola's court shahada was reduced to her charges related to physical torture. It erased the charges related to sexual assault. This is a crime that is classified as rape in the Egyptian penal code (EIPR, 2016).

It is important to note that though Ola requested that the defendants in this case be handed the highest negative punishment, she strongly refused to hand them the punishment of execution. Ola is against capital punishment. She also insisted that the military police and state security forces be listed as a defendant, complicit in the crimes. However, this court refused her request.

Ola described to *Mada Masr*'s (Said, 2015) reporter what went on in the courtroom that day on April 21, 2015:

I was with Rami and my lawyer.

The defendants' lawyer, an Islamist, asked me, "You claim you were sexually assaulted?"

I responded, "Yes."

Then he asked, "How many hands were inside your pants? Did the assault happen from the back or the front?"

At this moment, I thought of screaming or insulting the lawyer with a few words. But I wanted to live with dignity. I did not want to break down and cry.

Instead of humiliating the lawyer, I responded by saying, "Honestly, when *you* get assaulted sexually, you will know it is very hard at such a horrifying moment to count how many hands are in your pants."

So, he responded, "I am a man, I would not be assaulted as such."

I said, "Not true, men like you do get sexually assaulted. I hope you do get sexually assaulted to know and realize what it means."

He insisted and said, "No, impossible."

I spoke back, "Yes, it happens frequently. And by the way, at the beginning of the detention, they sexually assaulted me not realizing I am not male."

Their lawyer responded in disbelief, "*No*, this did not happen."

At that moment, many in the audience and judges were laughing. But one of the accused Islamist leaders standing inside the cage in the courtroom was gesturing to their lawyer to stop his argument there. I continued, "Yes, of course it happens. Check the back of your pants and think about what might happen in that area." I was trying to raise my voice to have the Islamist leaders in the cage hear me.

On October 23, 2016, the cessation court, an interpretative high court in Egypt, confirmed the final decision of the criminal court of Cairo, charging Egyptian ex-President Mohammed Morsi and 14 of his assistants with "flaunting force (thuggery), illegally detaining protestors and physically torturing them" on December 5–6, 2012 (EIPR, 2016). They were not charged with the killing of the ten people who died during the incident and around the palace. They were sentenced to 20 years in prison.

At that point, and since the beginning of the January 25 Revolution, there were no charges dealt to any police, security, or military forces indicted with killing or wounding peaceful protestors.[11] The final verdict in Ola's court case excluded the charging of the military police, the central security forces, and the special presidential guard forces. They were participants or active facilitators of the crimes (and of killing ten people). Such a trial and verdict were part of the forces countering the Revolution and a clear persistent judicial pattern since the toppling of Mubarak on February 11, 2011. It represented the partial or selective and politicized justice of the moment (EIPR, 2016).

With this, Ola's court case was closed.

6 | THE POWER OF THE SHAHADAT: A LEGITIMATE ARABYYA FEMINIST METHODOLOGY AND A STRATEGY OF EXPOSURE AND RESISTANCE

If I had not taken them to court and stayed silent, what happened to me could have happened to any other Egyptian girl. (Samira)

I began to think of a strategy to come out publicly with my shahada. I know it was a hard decision to make, but I must do it. Because this violence has to stop. Not another woman must be hurt. (Yasmine)

They must know that they cannot break my soul. (Ola)

I offer three main claims about the power of the shahadat in this book. First, I reflect upon the legitimacy of shahadat as an Arabyya feminist research methodology. Next, I discuss how the power of shahadat builds on the three truths of bodily oppression, refusal, and fearlessness. To close, I discuss my analysis of the impact of the shahadat. Then I highlight their use as strategies of exposures and resistance on the ground of suwret yanayer.

Shahadat as a Legitimate Arabyya Research Methodology

Having dwelled with the tremendous power of Samira, Yasmine, and Ola's shahadat, having translated and represented them, having been transformed myself through this relational research, I now reflect on the hybridized shahadat~haki as a legitimate nasawyya Arabyya methodology. Using shahadat~haki in this study was a powerful and creative way of knowing by which Egyptian women divulged their experiences of state-sanctioned gendered at a vital moment in their lives and the crucial Revolution of 2011. These were actions of theorizing from the bodies of women themselves. They expressed accumulations of Egyptian women's visceral knowledge. I hope that my use of Samira, Yasmine, and Ola's shahadat as an Arabyya methodology in this study adds to the "diversity of approaches among women academics in/from the Arab region" (El Said et al. 2015, p. 6) and in some way furthers our theorizing about women's contribution to the Egyptian January 25 Revolution.

Using shahadat of Egyptian women, translating them, and developing textual narratives might form the basis of a larger solidarity-centered transnational feminist praxis using Arabyya and Chicana feminist methodologies. For myself, this has been an intentional academic and political act between an Arabyya feminist in North America with women in Egypt. It has involved foregrounding the hybrid and complex lived experiences of women in Egypt to counter the compartmentalized and sensationalized forms of representation that have proliferated in Western media. It has also been my direct response to Samira, who expressed her skepticism of Western media, and researchers who want to write about Egyptian women. Furthermore, shahadat–haki are Arabyya methodologies because they do the urgent work of bridging "individuals with collective histories of oppression" (Delgado Bernal et al., 2012, p. 364) in order to re-center people's ways of knowing and elicit social change globally. It is the work of collaborations and dynamic alliances between activists on the ground and academics in the universities, between Arabic and English, and between the people in Egypt and the people in the United States.

At the core of this study, my translation of the shahadat was crucial in the construction of an oppositional and theorizable testimonial text (Reyes & Rodríguez, 2012). The outcome of this translation allowed me and the shaahedat to speak back to the ways the U.S. academy, corporate media, and Western think tanks produce and disseminate knowledge about Arab women in the Egyptian Revolution (El Said et al., 2015). Translation from Arabic was an ongoing and urgent political praxis (Castro & Ergun, 2017) necessary in exploring the power of Egyptian women's shahadat. It also opened political possibilities "to grow an alliance of transnational actors" (Nagar, 2014, Kindle locations 2923–2926) between myself and the three shaahedat. Thus, the translation of the women's shahadat from Arabic into English was my act of solidarity meant to respond to "the global processes that serve as recolonizing practices" (Trinidad Galván, 2014, p. 138).

My process of translation sought, as Tissot (2017) writes, to "challenge the power hierarchies inherited from centuries of oppression and resistance" (p. 29). Additionally, I have simultaneously translated the Arabic text of the shahadat themselves and the context within and after suwret yanayer. This process of contextualization, I suggest, can deepen our questioning and exposure of anti-revolutionary forces globally and locally. Thus, contextualizing through translation, Arab women's experiences became possible and present in and outside the Arabic-speaking context of suwret yanayer.

I would hope that shahadat~haki may become recognized as methodologies long needed by Arabyya feminists. These methodologies can counter the imperial and racist feminist knowledge in North America that essentialized Egyptian women before and after suwret yanayer. Doing this kind of Arabyya feminist praxis across languages, scholarships, and activisms (Nagar, 2014) is an invitation to English readers to enter an urgent and critical dialogue about the shahadat and the complexity they reveal about the contribution of Egyptian women in suwret yanayer. At the same time, the shahadat~haki are methodologies that can become core for transnational feminist struggles that seek to engage in the interlinked decolonizing knowledge productions (Naber, 2011).

The Power of the Shahadat

The power of shahadat builds on the three truths of bodily oppression, refusal, and fearlessness. First, these shahadat conveyed truths of Samira, Yasmine, and Ola's experiences of systemic state-sanctioned violent practices targeting women's bodies in public spaces, specifically at an intense moment of rebellion. They exposed truths about the specific criminal tactics of state-organized violence placed on women's bodies after suwret yanayer. Another way to say this is that the shahadat are powerful because they exposed realities about the foundational patriarchal logic of the militarist, Islamist, neoliberal, and neocolonial nexus that targets women's bodies to break dissent, political or social. As they exposed the logic of the regimes in power, they also exposed overlapping and entrenched gendering discourses within non-regime political parties and among some of the revolutionary men, family members, and friends. All of them are still insisting, willingly or not, to control and discipline the bodies of Egyptian women through their dress, as well as their mobility and presence in political public spheres (Hamzeh, 2011).

Second, the shahadat of Samira, Yasmine, and Ola are truths of refusal and defiance. They are refusals to hide their truth. They are their refusal to be silenced and forgotten. They are their insistence to bluntly reveal the truths in public, and hence to serve a clear political intention. Samira, Yasmine, and Ola refused to be silenced. Their shahadat were refusals to mediate their agency through any male-designated authority, political or social, that maintained the patriarchal dominance (Abouelnaga, 2015). They were a clear defiance to the networks of power and technologies that tried to silence them. Moreover, they refused to omit anything of their shahadat or to trivialize their meanings.

Finally, the fearless act of giving shahadat was ignited by the boldness of the protesters and activists in that moment as they faced the regime's immense violent machine. Both shaahedat and their shahadat were already immersed in suwret yanayer. Samira, Yasmine, and Ola embodied a newly discovered state of fearlessness created by the momentum of the moment. At the beginning of the revolutions in the Arab world in 2010 and 2011, many realized that those in the streets who were facing death, torture, disabilities, and mutilation had totally overcome any fear. This state of fearlessness was a distinct element of suwret yanayer. Accordingly, each of the shaahedat fearlessly spoke her truth against the dominant forces of the time—the Egyptian army and the Islamist president and their systems of repression. The shahadat of Samira, Yasmine, and Ola were also uniquely and additionally fearless because they broke a particular patriarchal narrative about women's bodies, a gendered shaming, and a social/familial "honor-tarnishing" discourse (Abouelnaga, 2015, p. 50).

Thus, the shahadat are powerful because they exposed the oppressive systems that targeted women and aimed to stop the people's revolution. The shahadat were evidence of Samira, Yasmine, and Ola's fight against the oppressive political and social systems of patriarchy, the foundation of counter revolutionary forces, and the nexus of militarism, Islamism, and societal traditions in the shifting revolutionary moments during 2011–2012. They offered a creative resistance tool specific to suwret yanayer. They were tools with which they confronted the massive military power of the Egyptian armed forces and the state security police, as well as the social powers of the Islamists and their militias. Finally, these powerful shahadat were embodied texts of women's undeniable contribution to/in the Egyptian January 25 Revolution of 2011, suwret yanayer.

Though these shahadat stand on their own and they speak for themselves in the previous chapters, here I open the space from my perspective, as an Arabyya feminist, to read their power. I discuss in more detail how the power of these shahadat was driven by their detailed graphic content, the strategic timing of making them public, and the media outlets they used to disseminate. I also share what impact these three shahadat made during the short two years after suwret yanayer, 2011–2012. I focus on their impact on the political and social realms, as well as on the social interactions of Egyptians in the public and on their private lives, including the personal impact on all three shaahedat.

In the next discussion, I specifically address the following questions: What were the strategies of resistance that gave these shahadat the power to become impactful across political, social, and personal contexts? What was their tangible impact on solidarity, the laws, and the collective conversation about violence against women? What did the experience of coming out in public with such powerful truths mean to each one of the shaahedat? What did each one of the women gain and sacrifice? At the end, I highlight the power of their legacy as archives, memory, and as Arabyya feminist research methodologies.

Shahadat as Strategies of Exposure and Resistance

Samira, Yasmine, and Ola's strategic use of content, timing, and choice of media outlet was deliberately meant to serve five main aims. Those aims were to maintain their dignity, stop violence against women, get justice, punish those responsible, and stop the counter revolutionary forces of the time.

Content of the Shahadat

The content of each shahada was a specifically implemented strategy to resist the transitional militarist and Islamist regimes that took over after suwret yanayer. This strategy was meant to counter the regimes' narratives about women and about suwret yanayer. The shahadat's content exposed the different state-orchestrated tactics of violence against women in the public sphere and their perpetrators and accomplices. They exposed the tactics of violence against women as systemic and organized by the regime, rather than random incidents.

Samira's shahada exposed the practices of kushoof el'uzryyah, Yasmine's shahada exposed mob rape, and Ola's shahada exposed sexual assault against women in detention. Together, Samira, Yasmine, and Ola exposed both systems of oppression, the militarist and the Islamist. They have particularly exposed the military forces, police forces, and militias, all of which were apparatuses that were complicit in the three terrorizing tactics against women after suwret yanayer. The shahadat of Samira and Ola exposed the perpetrators of violence against them by publicly identifying or naming them. They also exposed the designs of these state-organized tactics, their tools and aims, and the places where they occurred. This exposure was a strategy of resisting the silencing and erasures of people's lived experiences of state repression. It was a strategy that insisted on counter-ing the denial and deception narrative of the military and the Islamist regimes of the time.

It is important to note that counter revolutionary forces were working hard not only to erase the content of these shahadat altogether, but to specifically erase any sexual content in them. For example, Ola was clear about her intention to republicize her detailed shahada for two particular reasons. Though she made her initial shahada on social and mass media outlets, her experience of "sexual violation" was aggressively silenced by the court and unheard by her male comrades in the political party she was part of during suwret yanayer.

In the two legal cases she filed, Samira named Ahmed Adel Mohamed El Mougy as the main criminal conducting kushoof el'uzryyah. She named him as the military doctor who raped her and six other women. Samira also named General Abdel Fattah El Sisi, the head of the military intelligence services at the time, as the highest military commander who oversaw the military personnel who ordered kushoof el'uzryyah in the Huckstep military base. She named El Sisi as one of the members of SCAF, the de facto ruling body of the time. Samira's naming of the doctor, El Sisi, as well as the military base where she was detained and sexually assaulted, exposed those responsible for the crime of kushoof el'uzryyah.

On the other hand, Ola's shahada named those who were responsible for her detention and sexual assault on live TV and in the legal case she pursued. Ola specifically named Dr. Alaa Hamza of the Muslim Brotherhood, Mahmood Ibrahim, minister of interior, President Morsi himself, and General El Sisi, the minister of defense at the time.

Additionally, Samira, Yasmine, and Ola used detailed visual and graphic content as a strategy to strengthen the credibility of their shahadat. They were fully aware that they needed to compensate for the absence of visual evidence of the violence they experienced. None of the three incidents were accidentally or intentionally filmed or photographed like the incident of beating sit el banat, which was caught on camera. Sit el banat, who chose to stay anonymous, didn't need to speak out. The video and the photograph of a fully geared anti-riot police stomping sit el banat's half naked body spoke for her as solid evidence of the violence coordinated by the military regime. It was the visual that moved the collective consciousness of millions of Egyptians.

Hence, Samira, Yasmine, and Ola's detailed visual and graphic content of their experiences of specific state-sanctioned sexual violence was the solid proof they could provide. It was a content that made their shahadat more intelligible and more moving to the general public. Samira was clear about the necessity of this strategy when she stated:

> The challenge in this case is that people may not believe me or do not think my shahada is credible because I was not photographed at the time. (Ibrahim, 2011)

Timing of the Shahadat

Samira, Yasmine, and Ola consciously timed publicizing their shahadat. This timing was another strategy of resistance they used to counter the regimes' narratives about women and suwret yanayer. Samira publicly and fully shared her shahada about eight months after the incident, Yasmine after two months, and Ola a few hours after her assault. After her release Ola's friends took her to the hospital. Immediately after, she divulged her shahada live on TV with a badly bruised left eye (Foda, 2012).

Samira and Yasmine shared the first version of their shahadat with loved ones, family, and friends. This gave them the space to process the assault itself and consider the personal, social, and political ramifications if they stayed silent. Samira gradually shared the details of kushoof el'uzryyah with her father at home over a few days following her release. She was gaining her strength and processing with him her options to fight back. Additionally, the military regime made sure that the state-owned media closed all opportunities for Samira to publicly speak her truth immediately after the incident. Instead, for the next eight months, she shared it with her lawyers only.

When it became obvious to Samira that the regime was prolonging her legal case and while she was enduring threats by state security services and the censorship of the media for about eight months, she began to publicly share her shahada more frequently and with more details. Activists video-recorded her shahada to disseminate online and it was shared millions of times. Samira's timing to finally share her shahada publicly was also calculated as elmagles ela'la lilqwat almusalaha (SCAF) was getting more exposed and was losing its narrative about the military as *the* protector of suwret yanayer. This was almost a year before Yasmine was mob raped at the end of November 2012 and Ola was assaulted by the Islamist militias at the beginning of December 2012. Samira's shahada cultivated the ground for Yasmine and Ola to speak out more immediately after the assaults.

Yasmine, on the other hand, shared all the details of the horrific rape experience with her friend, Zainah, right when she was dropped off at her place after the 90-minute-long horrific rape. She did not want to forget any details. For two weeks, she kept recounting her shahada and asking artist and writer friends to publish her shahada, but they were paralyzed or reluctant. During this time, Yasmine's father strongly opposed her desire to appear on TV sharing her shahada. Yasmine came out with her shahada to the public in two phases, first anonymously, and then openly on live TV. On December 2, 2012, eight days after the incident, Yasmine asked a journalist friend to publish her words verbatim without mentioning her name on his Facebook account.

This shahada was republished on the website of mu'asasat almara' aljadeedah [New Woman Foundation][1] on December 3, 2012 (New Woman Foundation, 2012) then on the website of Nazra lilderasat alnasawyya [Nazra for Feminist Studies][2] on January 23, 2013 (Nazra for Feminist Studies, 2013). Yasmine named this as "the anonymous testimony" in which her friend identified her as "my friend Y." By the end of January 2013, Yasmine realized that mob rapes were increasing exponentially; therefore, she decided to spill out her shahada with all its details on a live TV show (Abdel Hafeez, 2013; Balba, 2013; EIPR, 2013a).[3] Two months after the incident, on February 1, 2013, Yasmine shared her shahada live on TV for 12 consecutive minutes and the public all over Egypt listened (Saa'd, 2013).

This was the first shahada in which Yasmine identified herself, facing the Egyptian public live on TV. She showed her ripped clothes to emphasize the brutality of the assault. After this particular shahada, civil society and women's organizations, as well as other media outlets, invited Yasmine to share her shahada many more times. Every time she had a platform, she would add more details to the shahada along with her analysis, telling listeners what it meant to her and how it fit into the moment Egypt was living in the aftermath of suwret yanayer.

The time of revealing the shahadat was also connected to the particular circumstances when each assault happened. The two years after suwret yanayer was a dynamic time of resistance with multiple and fluid ways of expression. This time period opened fissures to push back, speak up, and resist as the Revolution was still alive in the street and the regime was scrambling to hold onto its narrative and its power. First, the divulging of the sha-hadat, starting with Samira, was marked by the beating of sit el banat on December 16, 2011, which was captured on camera. That moment/incident suddenly and very vividly exposed the transitional military regime. Though the military regime was trying to minimize the price it had to pay with all sorts of fail-ing public relations and media tactics, the violence against sit el banat signaled another increase and a second tactic of state-sanctioned violence against women.

The visibility of the violence against women in this incident intensified the resistance of the people and emboldened Samira while she was still fighting her case in military courts and had just shared her shahada with a couple of revolutionary collec-tives or civil rights organizations. Second, Ola's and Yasmine's revealing of their shahadat was also driven by a specific intense moment of transition, when state-sanctioned violence peaked at the Itihhadyyah events and the second anniversary of suwret yanayer—the end of 2012 and the beginning of 2013. This moment was clearly marked by mob rapes and sexual assaults in makeshift detention spaces, two other tactics of violence against women. State-sanctioned violence against women took another turn with the Muslim Brotherhood assuming power first in the parliament at the end of 2011 and then with the presidency of Morsi in June 2012. It increased exponentially when Morsi was struggling to consolidate powers by the end of November and people were pushing back.

Thus, the timing of the shahadat was also catalyzed by the revolutionary moment of suwret yanayer itself, and simulta-neously energized it. This synergetic relationship between the shahadat and suwret yanayer happened in the context of the transitional military rule and the elected Islamist presidency and majority parliament. That is, it was facilitated by the continuous pull and push between the increased resistance of the people and the increased state-sanctioned repression of the people and violence against women. Additionally, the timing of disclosing the shahada was directly connected to confronting counter revolutionary forces. The shahadat were used as another revolutionary tool to resist the regimes' oppressive apparatuses, which were madly unleashed as soon as suwret yanayer started. The shaahedat used the timing of their public disclosure to confirm the revolutionary narrative calling for the mistrust in the transitional military rule and the elected Islamist government and president. They used the immediacy of informing the people about the incidents as a nonviolent tool against the brutal machine of the army, the Islamist militias, and the corrupt courts of the regimes.

Media Outlets of the Shahadat

The shaahedat were very deliberate in which media outlets the used. They had both local and far-reaching media outlets available to them, including spoken Egyptian Arabic, textual, visual, and auditory modes of expression that could address and reach thousands, if not millions, of people.[4] They used live TV shows on several privately owned stations, newspapers, Facebook, Twitter, and YouTube. Indeed, they were incredibly strategic in using live TV to urge the halt of the sexual violence and to amplify their call for justice.

Samira, Yasmine, and Ola reiterated their shahadat fully, or in pieces, in courts, on TV, and other social and political media outlets. They repeated their shahadat often on any outlet that opened up for them. They were driven by an unyielding persistence to expose the state-sanctioned violence against women, to stop the violence against women in all its forms, to get justice, and to maintain their dignity. They did not want one more woman to go through what they experienced. They wanted the perpetrators, and the system that supported them, to be punished. For example, Samira was deliberate about the aim of her shahada. She stated:

> When I decided to rebel, speak out, and expose the crime of kushoof el'uzryyah that I experienced with other women who were detained in an army prison, my main goal was to stop the violation of women's bodies by stopping kushoof el'uzryyah on any girl. And I succeeded. (Ibrahim, 2011)

Additionally, Yasmine made it clear why she continued to speak up. She said:

> I imagined that if I tell my story, people will sympathize. But this is not enough. I need to speak and speak because people did not see what happened to me. How can they sympathize or understand when they did not see? I get some energy knowing I can explain and help them understand. But if they do not understand that sexual assault and rape against women are crimes, then I will speak over and over to at least let people know what happened to me. (Khaled, 2017)

For example, when Samira was first interviewed live on OnTV, she repeated, at the beginning and at the end of the show, insisting on a statement she had on her Facebook page since March 2011:

> I will not give up my rights. I am calling on the Egyptian people, asking them to save me and to bring me justice. People of Egypt, save me from those oppressors. I am one of the People. I do not trust the army nor the prosecutor nor the judiciary all together. The people of Egypt will bring me my rights. (Ibrahim, 2011)

Reem Maged is one of very few journalists who intentionally opened the space on her live TV show for women and the revolutionists to give their shahadat. Reem Maged added:

This is an obvious shift from random individual incidents to organized group attacks, in daylight, in public places. They are not differentiating between who the target is, they are not selecting which women get attacked. They are attacking all kinds of women, those wearing a hijab or niqab or not, foreigner or Egyptian, young or old. (Balba, 2013)

The decisions Samira, Yasmine, and Ola made about the content, the timing, and the media outlets to disseminate these shahadat, while spontaneous, were also very strategic and their impacts recognizable. These strategies of resistance gave the shahadat power and charged their impact politically, socially, and personally.

Political, Social, and Personal Impacts of Shahadat

The impact of these shahadat on the political and social lives of Egyptians in the two years after suwret yanayer played out on several interconnected fronts.

Feminist and Intersectional Solidarity

The shahadat of Samira, Yasmine, and Ola exploded into unprecedented women-led demonstrations in Egypt, as well as a number of virtual campaigns and solidarity demonstrations around the Arab world—thawret al mar'a al Arabyya [Revolution of the Arab Woman].[5] They also mobilized popular solidarity movements and campaigns and pressure groups addressing sexual violence against women, such as quwet dhid altahharaush/alia'tida' elgamai [Operation Anti-Sexual Harassment/Assault (OpAntiSH)],[6] shoft tahharaush (I Saw Harassment, n.d.), and khareettat etahharaush eljinsi [Harassmap][7] (Harassmap, n.d.). They helped shape legal, civil, and human rights alliances, which in turn helped women in their legal cases. The shahadat also created and energized an intersectional solidarity block of feminists and women activists, journalists, doctors, writers, and artists.

Everyone in solidarity with Samira, Yasmine, and Ola was convinced, like they were, that "silence is not an option, it is not acceptable" (Balba, 2013). Speaking in public—without fear and with exceptional courage—the shahadat of these women were catalytic to mobilizing two unprecedented major women protests in 2011–2013. Yasmine said:

> Women were fighting to stay in the center and on the forefront of essuwra. Cairo had two major women's marches, on December 20, 2011, after the world saw how Egyptian military personnel attacked protestors and beat, dragged, and stripped sit el banat in the streets. It was also a response to kushoof el'uzryyah. (El Baramawy, personal communication, October 2017)

On February 6, 2013, another huge women's march was organized to protest the mob rapes orchestrated by the state systems, both military and security forces, right after the second-anniversary celebrations of suwret yanayer. With several civil society organizations and campaigns, both marches were calling for the end of sexual violence against women (El Baramawy, personal communication, October 2017).

The solidarity which emerged at this time sustained Samira, Yasmine, and Ola through their struggle against the regimes, in the courts and the streets, and against the society, at home. Samira, for example, literally carried the power of this solidarity when she walked into the courtroom surrounded by dozens of supporters on March 16, 2012. Samira carried a banner that said "You cannot break me" before hearing the final verdict on her case in March 2012. This statement referred to Samira, herself and her shahada, facing the might of the Egyptian military and the bias of the military court. It also referred to the power of the critical mass of bodies next to her. This statement asserted the power of the collective, the people fighting together on all fronts to sustain their revolution.

Unapologetic Language about Gendered Violence

The shahadat encouraged a new and unapologetic language about sexual violence against women, as well as more daring conversations and robust discussions on live TV and in private circles. Particularly, the shahadat shaped the dynamic of the public political conversation about violence against women. They opened new "discursive spaces" and presented a "language of its own" (Abouelnaga, 2015, p. 41). That is, the shaahedat constituted a new language, using new words to make sense of this gendered violence to themselves and to make it intelligible to the public. With this language, the shaahedat refused the common discourse about sexual harassment as merely a mild assault in words or touching. They refused the use of the generalizing and evasive term "harassment." Instead, they used the words "kushoof el'uzryyah," "rape," and "sexual assault."

As a result, the language about shame and the blame of women began to shift. Yasmine repeated this in many ways and on different occasions:

The [assaulted] woman is not the shame or the shameful. She is not the one who is guilty, she is not the one who committed the crime. Women got used to being silent about their bodies and were made to feel devalued and ashamed. On the other hand, men who express their sexuality in any form are characterized as brave and they get rewarded for it. I never at any point felt ashamed or responsible for it. (El Baramawy, 2013)

Similarly, Samira was also trying to have the people see the double revolution women were in, one against the repressive regime and one against the repression of societal norms and constructions of women. She wrote to me, saying:

My revolution aims to free all of us women from society's shackles which make the woman a victim and a perpetrator simultaneously. (Ibrahim, personal communication, 2015)

They were using language that focused on the systemic violence instead of victim-blaming language focusing on individuals. This new language refused to be silent about sexual violence—it refused the rules of what to say and what not to say. The language of the shahadat impacted the understanding of the violent gendered experiences as systemic and as a crime. The language was accessible, and hence inspired thousands of other spontaneous shahadat to come out on social media, including live shows on non-state-sponsored TV stations.

The unapologetic language subverted the gendered violence in the governing regimes and political parties from the Islamist to the socialist. For example, Abouelnaga (2015) asserted that Samira Ibrahim:

> did not stick to the rule of the script triggered a hugely hostile social reaction. By smashing the myth of the female body as a symbol of personal and collective national honour and as a site of docility. Ibrahim and her generation were able to shift the major forms of violence and abuse practised on the female body to the political terrain. (p. 45)

By the end of 2012 and beginning of 2013, mob rapes against women in the public sphere around protests and peaceful rallies increased exponentially. Parallel to this increase of sexual violence, public conversations and campaigning against mob rape grew more intense and widespread on TV shows and on social media. This was guided by women in educational workshops and panel discussions run by civil rights and women's organisations. Discussions of the state-sanctioned violence against women and women's rights over their bodies became an everyday conversation, not in the privacy of homes, but out in the open and in every political space where women showed up. Such conversations unpacked details of the assaults and patterns in the assaults to help make sense of violence against women in this counter revolutionary moment. For example, on a live TV interview,

Dr. Magda Adli of El Nadeem Center for the Management and Rehabilitation of Victims of Torture and Violence shared the following analysis:

> During the 18 days of the Revolution none of this happened. It was straight after February 11, 2011, with the victory of the Revolution, organized thugs were unleashed in the streets. They are mercenaries, whether paid by the police state, the military regime, or the Islamists now. Learning from the latest testimonies shared with El Nadeem, we see a clear pattern. A big group of men, the mob, works by a plan of a systematic attack. Their job is to target a woman in public space, in revolutionary marches. They isolate one woman at a time. Then they form a cordon by the woman, herd her away from the crowd, and finally isolate her and circle tarp her to begin the attack. In the meantime, they are shouting here and there. One would say, "I will protect you," another "Leave her alone, she is my sister," and they make a lot of noise to drown her screams within the circle. (Balba, 2013)

The host of the show, Reem Maged, responded:

> The Ministry of Interior left the prisons without guards during the 18 days, and many of the imprisoned fled and were let loose or used later as thugs to disperse protests and turn them into a violent incident. Those thugs are directly connected to Mubarak's police state and their attempt to survive as Mubarak was forced to step down. The Islamists only maintained the use of thuggery to suppress the masses. They realized that reforming the police and ministry of interior won't work to their advantage. That is, they kept the police state as is to control people's resistance. It is needed to break the whole people rather than go after individuals. (Balba, 2013)

Within a short period after publicizing the shahadat, Samira, Yasmine, and Ola broke two myths: first, the nationalist and religious myths about the sanctified narratives of the Egyptian army and Islamic political groups and parties; and second, the weakness of women and women's bodies. They opened new spaces to speak back to counter revolutionary powers about women in the public sphere, the Revolution, and the revolutionaries. They subverted gendered violence instigated by the interlocked patriarchal forces of the regimes and society at large, and showed that the regime did not succeed in breaking their dignity and could not dehumanize Samira, Yasmine, and Ola.

In January 2013, on Reem Maged's show, Juana Joseph,[8] a member of Operation Anti-Sexual Harassment/Assault (OpAntiSH), said:

> Those thugs were psychologically programmed not to see women they are attacking as humans. For years they have been trained to demonize women. They were ready to be unleashed. At the same time, the society was reactive and ready to tell women to stay at home. I am saying, the society with its norms is ready to maintain the construction of women as objects, things. Women will not take a better position in this society unless we stop depending on men to save us. We need a societal struggle to change the normative values and practices about the shaming and blaming of women. Because they know the Revolution would not have happened without the women of Egypt. Without women there is no Revolution. And they do not want the Revolution to continue, reach its goals. They tried to terrorize women, but women were not afraid and were not deterred. They were insisting to fight this battle. (Balba, 2013)

The language of the shahadat and the resulting discursive shift showed their impact on the legal and the artistic realms. Presenting the shahadat of Samira and Ola in both military and civil courts shifted the legal debate on sexual violence against women. When Samira courageously filed the lawsuit against elmagles ela'la lilqwat almusalaha (SCAF), she was the first to break the silence against sexual harassment and rape (Abouelnaga, 2015). In two separate cases, Samira sued SCAF and the conscript doctor,

Ahmad Adel Mohamed El Mougy, who conducted a vaginal violation on her. Though SCAF banned the practice of kushoof el'uzryyah in December 2011, Samira lost the two cases. All of the officers and the doctors involved were acquitted. This was a 15-month-long court battle.

Ola's challenging shahada about the Islamists' use of sexual violence to break women further aggravated people's mistrust in the Muslim Brotherhood and the unviability of Islam in politics. The legal shahadat of Samira and Ola contributed to changes in the law and the drafting of the new constitution in 2014. Two tangible legal outcomes of these shahadat were the criminalization of sexual assault and rape, and the discussions and crafting of the new constitution (2011–2014).

As the shahadat were read and circulated, they were represented artistically in graffiti, comics, paintings, caricatures, and other art forms, further mobilizing the local and Arab solidarity movements. They became part of the conversation of public dissent escalating in different forms and several spaces (aamiry-khasawnih, 2018). Artists and their public murals and graffiti in the streets created and responded to the new language of the shahadat. For example, the slogan about Yasmine's bravery to speak out was presented in a huge banner with her face and long curly hair saying, "bttalatna mish haykhlassu."[9] In English, this slogan may translate to "our sheroes are many and endless," "our sheroes will not die," "our sheroes will always rise," or "we have many sheroes present/among us." This slogan is not only giving credit to Yasmine for speaking up about organized mob rapes, but to the thousands of women who made suwret yanayer and continued to struggle for its aims.

The widespread graffiti telling the story of suwret yanayer included many unique representations of Samira's shahada exposing the crimes of the armed forces and SCAF. Walls in Cairo and other cities in Egypt were filled with graffiti of Samira's face along with statements saluting her courage and emphasizing that the military cannot break women's will. Hundreds of stenciled images of Samira's recognizable face looking up and forward with dignity gave her campaign momentum. Those images, sometimes juxtaposed with slogans refusing assaults on women's bodies, became symbols of Egyptian women's power and acknowledgment of their important active role in suwret yanayer. Other graffiti images depicted her face above a tank surrounded by military personnel mixed with faces of the doctor who conducted kushoof el'uzryyah; these images were also mobilized and made visible people's understanding of state-sanctioned sexual violence against women and their support of the rallying calls of Samira, Yasmine, and Ola. The continuous struggle for the aims of suwret yanayer and women's rights to their bodies and access to the public sphere were furthered by artists' and people's support of Samira. Thus, the shahadat worked hand in hand with people's creative and spontaneous expressions against the entrenched regimes of power using graffiti, posters, banners, chants of slogans in the streets, holding testimonial public sessions, and panel discussions.

Personal Sacrifice

During the two years after suwret yanayer, Samira, Yasmine, and Ola paid an immeasurable and multilayered personal price and made immense sacrifices. First, each one of the shaahedat endured the bodily trauma and the consequential emotional trauma fighting for justice. Additionally, each one of them took on new and huge responsibilities that they did not plan or wish for.

Samira: "Kushoof el'uzryyah was a nightmare."

Samira's experience of kushoof el'uzryyah marked the beginning of the end of the Revolution and the start of a dramatic change in her life and in Egypt. After a 15-month-long legal battle, Samira struggled to get back to her "normal" life. She stated to me when I first met her in 2015 that the past three years were the most difficult in her life. She also wrote, "Yes, I paid a high personal price for my fight to succeed against the society. As a result, I lost my reputation and job" (Ibrahim, personal communication, 2015). This was a low point in the revolutionary struggle when many of Samira's comrades of suwret yanayer were detained and as President El Sisi grabbed power and his repressive regime ran rampant.

To Samira, kushoof el'uzryyah was a "nightmare that threatened Egyptian women" (Ibrahim, personal communication, 2015). Samira's fight was not about the nightmare she was going through, but her concern about other women getting coerced into kushoof el'uzryyah. Knowing that the Revolution was an ongoing fight against the repressive militarist regime and its systemic attempt to terrorize women out of the public sphere, she was driven to guarantee the banning of this violence. That is, as soon as she came out with her shahada, Samira took a major responsibility to challenge the state power, as well as endure the entrenched social forbiddance on behalf of many other women who did not, or could not, speak out. Samira wrote:

> Kushoof el'uzryyah were not only a threat to those women who were resisting the governing regime, but also those who were arrested for other reasons. They were afraid of societal implications because exposing anything related to sex is an offense to societal normative practices and rotten inherited traditions. They were afraid because even if they were exposing a crime, the society would still protest their truth and blame them. They would pay a double price taking on the crime and being both the offenders and the victims at the same time. (Ibrahim, personal communication, 2015)

Samira refused to succumb to two major patriarchal powers by stating:

> When I spoke out, I was not only revolting against the society and its norms, but also challenging the Egyptian regime, represented in this case by the military establishment itself and

the complicit individual army officers. I was rebelling against what was taken for granted or considered the right of the regime and the society, both of which are built on patriarchal logics. My revolution is not only against the repressive and corrupt regime and its army, but also against the whole society. My revolution is against the patriarchal society and all its patriarchal unquestioned traditions. My revolution is against those two powers hiding behind the masks of protecting Egypt and its women. The aim of my revolution is to liberate myself and us, women, and break both chains. (Ibrahim, personal communication, 2015)

That is, Samira's double struggle was against "modern patriarchal values, set implicitly by society and consolidated crudely by the state" (Abouelnaga, 2015, p. 40). It was about women being reduced "to the corporeal body by which abuse, mutilation, isolation and harassment were justified culturally" (Abouelnaga, 2015, p. 40). Early on in 2012, Samira stated:

Rape and sexual assault are key tools [to break women] so it is a major part of women's struggles. I also think traditional political movements are not helping women. I work in the streets [on the ground] with women's issues in my city of Sohag. I have seen Islamists harassing a poor woman making a living from selling vegetables on the streets. They shouted, "Go and get dressed modestly." In response, she was so angry that she took of her shirt and was screaming back at them. She is a model of a hard-working Egyptian woman who has been betrayed by traditional political representatives. Women have been betrayed by the Islamists, the leftists, and the liberals. She is fighting on her own, working hard for a living in public, then at home at the end of the day. She is solely standing against the hegemony of the Islamists. Women are abused and used in politics.

What I am saying here is that we need to speak out from those places on the bottom with people there, and not speak from the top at people in lower positions. To act for and with women, we need to put our hand on the pain and feel the pain. I am also referring here to kushoof el'uzryyah case. Speaking out has encouraged girls to speak out themselves if they were sexually harassed and report to the police. Previously, they would be afraid to report, and now they are unafraid. I get stopped in the streets and girls tell me, "Thank you for teaching us to report at the police station and report on what happens to us." The case of kushoof el'uzryyah had a far-reaching political impact because it reflected the humiliation Egyptian women [had to endure] and the oppression [they live]. (Akhbar El yom TV, 2012)

Importantly, through pursuing her rights in the court, Samira was fully aware that it meant publicly sharing she was raped or she may have "lost" her virginity.[10] Exposing such a personal truth could shame any woman and stop her from fighting back. This is what the military regime was betting on. However, all three women consistently stated that the shame and the wrong was done by the state forces, not them. To show how they turned around the language, and hence the public discourse and understanding of their calls, it is helpful to turn to the meaning of the word "shame" in Arabic.

Shaming, the shameful, or the wrong is 'ar[11] in Arabic. The root verb 'ara[12] means exposing of a body part or made nude (Baheth, n.d.). It also means destroyed or spoiled (Baheth, n.d.). This is to say that Samira, Yasmine, and Ola were clearly exposing the military and Islamist regimes or stripping them of their masks. As a result, they turned the shame and shaming on the perpetrators. They also turned the shame, associated with the assault inflicted on them, to discredit those who actually assaulted them. They turned around the normative narrative of shaming women, which is meant to objectify, sexualize, and destroy them, onto the perpetrators of the crimes. Samira, Yasmine, and Ola refused to be criminalized for being in the streets fighting for the Revolution's aims.

Though they paid a personal price, Samira, Yasmine, and Ola exposed the wrongdoing, the shame of the Egyptian army and the Islamist regime who normalized sexual violence against women. They exposed society's logic that renders women as objects or good for marriage only if they are virgins. They stripped the mask off the face of the military institution as the protector of suwret yanayer and the Egyptian people and men as protectors of women. They uncovered the criminal practices of the military institution and the society. With this huge leap, all three women were fully aware of the high societal price they would pay as a result.

Sherene Seikaly (2013) clearly acknowledged that:

> Samira did not claim the category of the Virgin as a sacred space of refuge. She did not fight her brutalization in the tired terms of honor and righteousness. She fought it on political grounds. She confronted the precipice at which her flesh and its openings had become the terrain of public scrutiny, and defying descent she decided instead to walk all over it. At the same time, Samira challenged the societal rules by fighting the most powerful institution in Egypt.

The journalist Reem Maged asked Samira if her family were contemplating any social consequences, especially her chances to get married, given that she is the eldest with two other younger sisters and one brother. Samira responded:

> My mom thought of it, I am sure. However, my father responded to this as a challenge, and was supporting me throughout to restore my rights and stop this wrong. But my mom is kind and was affected. Moreover, this incident worked to my advantage. Those who are in my circle were very supportive, my friends, relatives were very sympathetic. This support started even before this case became public and I was visible and a public figure.

> Nobody in Sohag used the discourse of shame and shaming because I spoke out. On the contrary, most people were supportive of my stand and of filing the legal case. Though,

some do not believe that the army would do such a thing. Or they are in shock that the army have done something like this. (Ibrahim, 2011)

Samira paid a personal price within the first year after she was subjected to kushoof el'uzryyah. She was constantly threatened with more sexual assaults, death, and defamation. Her phone was tapped, and she received anonymous calls forcefully asking her to pull her report to the prosecutor. Additionally, a month after the military courts acquitted the doctor accused of performing kushoof el'uzryyah, Time magazine named her one of the world's 100 most influential people of 2012 (Theron, 2012). This did not last long. In April 2013, Samira was caught in a Zionist–Israeli campaign accusing her of anti-Jewish, anti-Israeli, and anti-American tweets (Foxman, 2013). As a result, the U.S. State Department rescinded her International Women of Courage award a day before Michelle Obama was meant to hand it to her.

As a result of the contradictory messages Samira received by those two so-called acknowledgments of her courage and the Egyptians revolting against tyranny, she had to navigate her overlapping subject positions facing the blunt brutality of the Egyptian army and its imperial funder, the United States. She had to grapple with the attacks questioning her stance toward the United States at a specific moment in which anti-Semitism was conflated with criticism of the Zionist settler-colonial Israeli project in Palestine. Hence, it became apparent to her that governmental and corporate media-controlled acknowledgments are conditional as they implicitly required her to submit to the U.S. imperial role in the region and to erase the historic and current Israeli violence against Palestinians.

Samira paid the price in another context when she escaped an assassination attempt while she was running for local council elections in 2016. Her stand against the military in 2011 and 2012 continued to frame her as a threat to the military represented by the new reign of President El Sisi. With the enforcement of local and global counter revolutionary forces and the re-emerging regime threats to her and persistent activists, Samira stated to me that she had matured too fast:

> I changed a lot in four years, since the start of essuwra, I was 22 years old and now I am 60. What I lived through and what my generation experienced was surely not experienced by those who are 70 years old now. I have been experiencing pain for five long years. (Ibrahim, personal communication, 2015)

When I asked her how she sustains herself with this pain, she responded:

> My persistence is the stable element in [my] life. (Ibrahim, personal communication, 2015)

Every time I met with Samira over the past four years, she was independently working as a freelance writer/reporter, helping women in her town, and trying to find a stable direction for her life.

Yasmine: "I don't know how I should live with it, it's not a nice life companion. It is always there, eating my soul."

Yasmine's life took a turn away from her music as she had to participate in campaigns against gendered violence in Egypt specifically, as well as in the regional campaign thuwret almara' fil 'alam alarabi [Revolution of Women in the Arab World][13] and the global campaign Global Protests against Sexual Terrorism Practiced on Egyptian Female Protestors (El Baramawy, 2013). Her face became recognizable in public and she became an inspiring icon and a shero defending women's rights to their bodies. Her shahada was represented in protest banners, slogans, graffiti, and caricatures. The graffiti with her face and big long curly hair and the slogan "bttalatna mish haykhlassu" was painted on the walls of the governorate of Mansura. A huge banner in red, black, and white with her face and recognizable curly hair was also used in several protests with the slogan "kulina Yasmine El Baramawy" [we are all Yasmine El Baramawy].[14]

Her name and bravery were cited in several Arab women protests from Mauritania to Yemen. She represented the strength of women's spirits in the face of sexual violence. The slogan "qad tassel lijasadi lakinak abadan lan tahzima rauhi" [you may be able to reach my body, but you cannot defeat our souls][15] was inspired by Yasmine. Famous Egyptian caricaturist Doaa Eladl's drawing of abadan lan tuhzama rauhi [my soul will never be defeated, or never will you defeat my soul] was another reflection of the impact of Yasmine's shahada on artists (Eladl, 2017).

Yasmine's experience of mob rape in 2012 and the trauma she suffered as a consequence changed her life forever. Five years after this horrific experience, Yasmine posted on her Facebook page:

> I don't know how I should live with it, it's not a nice life
> companion. I can't get rid of it and I can't get used to it,
> although I managed to transform it into something useful, but it
> is always there, eating my soul.

The personal sacrifice and the ensuing emotional state in which Yasmine lives following her rape did not contradict with her commitment and struggle to end sexual violence against women. She continued to work "on the ground as a volunteer for the new campaign, Operation Anti-Sexual Harassment/Assault" (OpAntiSH, n.d.).

Ola: "I was beaten and wounded in 2011, so I knew what to expect."

Ola paid an emotional price due to the assault itself and her legal fight that dragged on for over three years, but more so because of her struggle with her comrades in socialist political circles.

Ola was already engaged in political activism before she was assaulted at the Itihhadyyah. A year after suwret yanayer and before the Islamist militias detained and sexually assaulted her, Ola was invited to speak at the Rosa Luxemburg Foundation on the discussion of "Arab Revolt: Opportunities and Limits of Civil Disobedience" in Dresden, Germany, on January 27–29, 2012. Though she has been politicized while working on the ground against the police state, struggling against all kinds of repression, and fighting for labor justice since 2005, she took on a more intense role since suwret yanayer began. Ola stated, "I was beaten and wounded in 2011, so I knew what to expect" (Rosa Luxemburg Congress, 2012).

Ola was invited to help global audiences make sense of suwret yanayer and theorize the connection of the Egyptians' latest uprising to global struggles for justice (Rosa Luxemburg Congress, 2012). In the discussion of the Arab Revolt in Dresden, she helped to describe who participated in the Revolution, which worked to debunk the myths and exoticization of the Revolution as a youth uprising and a Facebook phenomenon. She helped unpack the complexity of such a momentous and dense event, hoping to refute the reductive counter revolutionary forces and Orientalist narratives. She was aware of the need to keep historicizing and contextualizing suwret yanayer. She said:

> Yes, the youth, us, were the spark of the Revolution, at the start others mocked us, at the same time we were surprised by our own action … soon enough all generations were participating. I saw old men refusing to leave the frontlines and denying their physical limitations. I also witnessed very young boys and of course women on the frontlines and elsewhere. (Rosa Luxemburg Congress, 2012)

Ola's experience of sexual assault and the prolonged and complicated court case took a toll on her. Unlike Samira and Yasmine, she was not supported by specific campaigns related to state-sanctioned gendered violence. Her specific shahada about the sexual assault the Islamists and Morsi's militias inflicted on her was erased from the court case. As a result, Ola had to continue to fight this erasure on internal political and personal fronts. Thus, in terms of each woman's personal sacrifice, Samira's and Yasmine's lives turned a sharp corner as they became active on the ground to stop violence against women, while Ola continued her political engagement and activism with Egyptian socialist-leaning parties and coalitions and solidarity groups outside Egypt.

(In)conclusion

The shahadat of Samira, Yasmine, and Ola impacted the understanding and ways of doing intersectional solidarity, popularized the unapologetic language about sexual violence against women, flipped the shaming discourse onto the perpetrators in the regimes, and had a long-lasting mark on each of the three women, whether in their personal lives or in their public roles. This layered impact of the shahadat is a huge part of suwret yanayer and its continuation, which reverberated in the words of Nadia Kamel, an Egyptian filmmaker and writer:[16]

> The revolution is a huge social phenomenon that only happens rarely ... A revolutionary event and its impact is impossible to measure by its political impact ... This is to say that reducing the phenomenon of the revolution only to what is happening on the political theater is blinding and silencing the truth. The important question I am posing here is, "What happened to the individuals?" ... Individuals are in a state of serious observation, whether they celebrated or hated the Revolution, hence continuing the Revolution. (Kamel, personal communication, February 15, 2017)

Nadia Kamel emphasized here that essuwra mustamirah in Egypt and its impacts are ongoing too: "The Revolution itself was bigger than absorbing everyone ... [its] social impact was bigger than the capacities of everyone and still is. It is an impact that cannot be measured" (Kamel, personal communication, February 15, 2017). With this, Nadia Kamel also insisted that we must attend to people's stories, which reflect the impact of the Revolution on the social realm and on their own experiences.

Samira, Yasmine, and Ola's shahadat exposed the regime's two decades-long imposed silences over the reality of violence against women in Egypt. They exposed the complicity of societal values and practices with the militarist and Islamist organized attacks on women's bodies. Their shahadat then further legitimized an Arabyya methodology of knowing and exposing oppression. The power of shahadat in this project revealed the resistance, resilience, and hope in the collective to challenge and transform oppressive regimes and begin moving toward dignity, freedom, and social justice.

The shahadat of Samira, Yasmine, and Ola revealed their power as they gave access to three women's theorizing about the gendered state-sanctioned violence at a significant moment in the lives of the Egyptians and Arabs. The shahadat were their sense-making of a moment that lasted two years after suwret yanayer, when the Egyptians were insisting to stay in the streets continuing their Revolution. They were the shaahedat's own knowing of the immense forces targeting bodies of women present in public. They were their calls for justice in an intense political context when masses of Egyptians were in a warlike zone, confronting a repressive machine comprised of militarist and police regimes as well as Islamist militias.

These shahadat of women in suwret yanayer were both tools and practices of resistance built on an enormous charge of raw, visceral knowledge. They were accounts of the lived experiences of Egyptian women of state-sanctioned violence against their bodies. Samira, Yasmine, and Ola were major silence-breakers, and hence holders of knowledge of suwret yanayer. With their truth-telling, they theorized the different tactics and the context of the state-sanctioned violence against them.

For me, working with the three shaahedat over the past five years was an act of solidarity. In particular, this was a process of Arab-to-Arab transnational feminist solidarity. This work was an assertion of the new feminism that is embedded in revolution

(Badran, 2011). With my commitments and praxis in this project, I built "situated" solidarities with the narrators and communities in Egypt to contest the cross-border configuration of state-supported gendered violence (Nagar, 2014). These commitments were about being aware of vulnerabilities and risks that were not just intellectual and political, but also "affects" in my skin, my bone, my flesh, and in my deepest ethical core.

The legacy of the shahadat of Samira, Yasmine, and Ola, as well as their experiences of the brutal state-sanctioned violence after suwret yanayer, were summed up by Juana Joseph, a member of Operation Anti Sexual Harassment (OpAntiSH):

> We must put those women as crowns on our head, respect them and value their sacrifice, like we did with those wounded, shot in the eye, or killed during the Revolution, like Hararah, Malek and [martyrs like] Khaled Said. At least we must remember and acknowledge their value and their gift to us, because we may not be able to pay them back. They are carrying the dirt that we should have dealt with a long time ago. We are complicit no matter what. When they use knives, they want to kill and end women's presence in the public. It is intentional, it is a premeditated crime. (Balba, 2013)

Shahadat are calls for action to awaken the consciousness of the people everywhere to seek justice by the people for the people and beyond the state and the regimes holding power. To Samira, her shahada is a tool to bring justice.

هاتلي حقي يا شعب...

People [of Egypt], bring me my right.

NOTES

1 Women's Resistance in the Egyptian Revolution: Arabyya Feminist Methodologies

1 شهادات—plural of shahada or testimonio.

2 سَوْرة (ثَوْرة) يناير.

3 حسني مبارك—Hosni Mubarak was the Commander of the Egyptian Air Force during the war of 1973, Vice President of Egypt in 1975, and President of Egypt after the assassination of President Anwar el-Sadat in 1981. He was 83 when the revolution erupted. He was "the headman of a thirty-year regime of institutional paralysis, religio-moral hypocrisy, crony capitalism, and police atrocity" (Amar, 2013, p. 28).

4 ميدان التحرير—midan etahrir is the geographical center of Cairo and the epicenter of suwret yanayer.

5 "massive paramilitary antiriot police" (Amar, 2013, p. 25).

6 الشعب يريد إسقاط النزام (النظام)—people want the downfall of the regime.

7 عيش حُريّة عَدالة إجتماعيّه.

8 سميرة إبراهيم.

9 كشوف العزرية (العذرية).

10 ياسمين البرماوي.

11 غلا شهبا.

12 أسْوار—this is colloquial Egyptian Arabic for al thuwaar (الثّوار) in classical Arabic. It refers to those who participated in the revolution of 2011.

13 شهادة.

14 شاهدات. This plural form of shaaheda [شاهده] is not listed in major Arabic dictionaries. Instead, it follows the masculine noun, and it is listed in all Arabic classical dictionaries as shuhood [شهود] (Maajim, n.d.).

15 نَسَويّة عَرَبيّة.
عربيّة—Arabyya is not only an Arab woman but also an Arab feminist.
نسَويّة—Nasawyya (feminista) is the feminine noun for feminist.
نَسَويّ—nasawyy is the masculine noun for feminist.

16 سَوْرة (ثَورة) خمسه وعشرين يناير.

17 ال١٨ يوم.

18 إسْوَرة—this is colloquial Egyptian Arabic for al thuwrah (الثّورة) in classical Arabic. Its root verb is ثار—thara, which means to revolt or rise against something or someone.

19 الشرطة يوم.

20 يوم التنحي.

21 المجلس الأعلى للقوات المسلحة—SCAF was the transitional governing body after the toppling of Mubarak on February 11, 2011. It was the de facto ruler of Egypt at the time, and in reality a continuation of Mubarak's old regime.

22 جماعة الإخوان المسلمين.—Muslim Brotherhood Society is an Islamist political group with an international network. It was legally registered in Egypt right after the revolution as حزب الحرّية والعدالة, hizb al hurya wal a'dalah, Freedom and Justice Party. In December 2011, together with the Salafist parties, they "captured 60 percent of the seats in the [Egyptian] parliament" (Bayat, 2017, p. 148). In June 2012, Mohammed Morsi, a prominent member, became the first elected president of Egypt after suwret yanayer.

23 إسّوّرة مستمرّة.

24 Throughout, I use Arabic terms and names transcribed into Latin alphabets with lay and popular spelling. I also include the Arabic form of the terms in endnotes. To Mona Baker (2016), "Transcription is another form of translation in its own right, and as such always involves decisions that reflect the position of the transcriber/translator" (p. 13). Additionally, to me, what to transcribe and how to transcribe Arabic terms is an epistemological decision in which I bring Arabic to the English text of this book and to the English readers themselves. It is an intentional invitation to a new relationship between languages and peoples.

25 النّسويّات العربيّة.

26 حكي—casual talk or conversations built on the intimacy of trust.

27 From an interview at http://www.dhip.ps/narrative-can-face-world/.

28 شاهدة. In most Arabic dictionaries, it is listed beside the masculine noun shahed and it is not used in the examples explaining the term. It is also listed to mean "the earth" or "tombstone," not a female witness. It is also not used in the feminine plural form with an alef ta [ات].

29 صمود.

30 حكاية—what is told, narrated, or storied, whether it is real or imagined (Almaany, n.d.).

31 The Egyptians were protesting in the streets from January 25 to February 11, 2011, until Mubarak resigned and transferred his governing powers to the Supreme Council of the Armed Forces (SCAF).

32 عواصف الربيع.

33 Several Egyptian feminists as well as civil society and legal organizations were recording and archiving as much material as possible related to the revolution and human rights violation.

34 لا للمحاكمات العسكرية للمدنيين.

35 سلوى الحسيني جوده.

36 رشا علي عبد الرحمن.

37 مُصرّين.

38 ناديا كامل.

39 دعاء العدل.

40 أبدأ لن تُهزم روحي.

41 I am a second-generation Palestinian born in Jordan.

42 قوات أمن الدولة—state security forces, also used interchangeably with the shorter term أمن الدولة, state security, and with قوات الأمن المركزي, central security forces.

43 مركز النديم لتأهيل ضحايا العنف والتعذيب.

44 آمال فاروق.

45 كفاية، الحركة المصرية للتغير—kefaya, enough in Arabic, is the Egyptian Movement for Change (established 2004) (Shorbagy, 2007).

46 Nawal Ali later died 2009, before the African Commission for Human Rights found that the state of Egypt was at fault in 2013 (Carr, 2014).

47 نقابة المحامين.

48 الأربعاء الأسود.

49 د. عايدة سيف الدولة.

50 ريم ماجد.

51 د. ماجدة عدلي.

52 الأمن المركزي—قوات الأمن المركزي—central security forces is used interchangeably with المركزي, central forces, and with أمن الدولة, 'amn edwallha or state security forces.

53 الشرطة العسكرية.

54 المتحف الوطني—also known locally as elmat-haf المتحف [the Museum] or المتحف المصري elmat-haf elmasri [the Egyptian Museum].

55 رشا عزب.

56 فحوصات العذرية—virginity tests.

57 المجمع العلمي.

58 ست البنات.

59 أحداث مجلس الوزراء — the events of the Cabinet Council.

60 This study was approved by the New Mexico State University Internal Review Board. Additionally, Samira, Yasmine, and Ola gave their consent to publish their public shahadat as well as what they shared with me directly. They have approved the testimonial text of their shahadat in the three core chapters of this book.

61 In her interview with Basem Yousef (2012), Samira Ibrahim said, "I know who this woman is, she is a university student and an A student. She is respectable and trustworthy and very educated. She is calm like an angel. She is religious and wears the cloak and a shawl and the headscarf. I met her around the first

Mohammed Mahmood St. protests (November 2011) where she was injured by a bullet. She was always carrying the Qur'an in her hands and walking slowly. She also was supportive and stood by me during my struggle in the legal case against the army. She would always be waiting for me early before the 9 a.m. court session outside the national security building. I know she is afraid to appear on media because she is college student and is worried that national security will harass or harm her. Or do anything to her. They may do horrible things to her. She is afraid to identify herself. Her main goal is to complete her degree [higher education]."

62 المليونيات—million people marches.

63 حزب النور السلفي—Annour Salafist Party is a revivalist Islamist movement and "part of a heterogenous entity—some preferred the status quo, others focused on enhancing the ethical self, while still others embraced a militant *takfiri* path—the sporadic and violent [moralizing] intrusions into free expression, artistic products, and women's rights" (Bayat, 2017, p. 152).

64 قصر الإتحادية للرئاسة—the executive headquarters of the Egyptian president.

2 Introducing the Three Shaahedat: Samira, Yasmine, and Ola

1 مكتبة ديوان—Diwan Bookstore (& Cafe).

2 صوهاج—the rural South Nile city of Sohag, about 400 km away from Cairo.

3 الجبل الأحمر.

4 الجمعية الوطنية للتغير.

5 Ola was born in 1981 and she is from Cairo.

6 حزب التحالف الشعبي الإشتراكي.

7 تيار التجديد الاشتراكي.

8 مجموعة العمل العمالي.

9 مصنع طنطا للكتان—City of Ttantta Linen Factory.

10 مصنع السويس للغاز—Swais Natural Gas Factory.

3 Shahada by Samira Ibrahim: Military-Sanctioned Kushoof El'uzryyah

1 The wording "madam or miss" is used to differentiate between those who are or have been married and those who have not been married. However, it basically intends to distinguish between those women who are sexually active from those who are not, inside or outside a marriage. Egyptian social and religious norms consider extramarital sex forbidden and unacceptable, especially for women.

2 أحمد عادل محمد الموجي.

3 .مركز هشام مبارك للقانون

4 .المبادرة المصرية للحقوق الشخصيّة

5 Khaled Said is a young man who was brutally tortured and killed by the police in 2010. Photos of his beaten-up and dead body sparked the Revolution, beginning with protests on Police Day, January 25. Those threats to Samira insinuated that the secret police could end up kidnapping her and killing her if she does not retract her indictment case against the military.

6 On January 29, 2012, Samira was summoned to the military court for an exceptional short meeting. On February 6, 2012, women prison guards were heard as witnesses. On February 13 and 20, 2012, the director of the military prison and doctors were heard as witnesses. On February 26, 2012, civil society and human rights defenders presented the results of their investigations.

4 Shahada by Yasmine El Baramawy: State Security-Sanctioned Mob Rapes

1 This was a commonly used phrase during suwret yanayer to calm the protestors and to de-escalate the violence and curb chaos.

2 The rapists and kidnappers all had penknives, big knives, wooden sticks, and belts (Yasmine haki with Manal, October 2017).

3 The men commissioned to do the mob rapes followed a specific plan. They slowly cordoned a woman away from her friends, then circled her and started the assault while shouting to drown out her screams. Lighting a fire torch at night around the woman assaulted was part of the pattern of this tactic. The torch was made of a wood stick with combustible material or a powerful gas blowtorch. This was also used to scare people away from the spot of the assault.

4 The distance from Mohammed Mahmoud Street to the area of Abdeen via Bab Ellouq is about 2 km, or a ten-minute ride.

5 Later, Yasmine realized that her friend Leila ended up there after the mob attack.

6 .لحظة خزعبليّة

7 Dr. Ahmed Harara, who was shot in two different incidents when Egyptian protestors were still targeted by Mubarak's security forces then the military regime's forces. Birdshot in the face, neck, and lungs, he lost the vision in his right eye on January 28, 2011, two days after he joined the Revolution, fighting for the toppling of Mubarak's 30-year-old regime. On November 19, 2011, he was on the frontlines of Mohammed Mahmoud Street, Battle I, when his left eye was targeted with a rubber bullet. He lost his vision in his second eye then. He became one of the Revolution's icons. Before getting blinded, he was a dentist.

5 Shahada by Ola Shahba:
Islamists-Sanctioned Sexual Assault

1 Rami is Ola's comrade from the Socialist Popular Alliance Party (حزب التحالف الشعبي الإشتراكي.). She is his leader/superior.

2 فلول—an Egyptian Arabic colloquial term that was used to describe the "remnants" of the previous regime. This word became popular after the Revolution, describing those who worked inside Mubarak's regime and his dismantled party, the National Democratic Party, and sustained his regime as businesses, individuals, and institutions.

3 This is a reference to Hamdeen Sabahi, at the time the leader of the Egyptian Popular Current, a pro-Revolution movement. He ran against Morsi in 2012 at the first presidential elections after the January 25 Revolution.

4 شريعة الله—Allah's law or God's way.

5 A leader of the Egyptian Popular Current—التيار المصري الشعبي.

6 غنيمة—Battle spoils.

7 محمد البلتاجي—Mohammed El Biltagi was at the time the secretary general of the Freedom and Justice Party (the Muslim Brotherhood's official party), third in the party's chain of command.

8 Muslim Brotherhood militias captured and beat women that day. They considered them infidels or apostates, non-Muslims. Rania Mohsen stated that they told her as they were ripping her headscarf off, "Infidels do not wear the hijab. This is our way of sacrificing and offering to our god [thinking they are in a religiously driven war]. At the same time, the military forces were shouting at me, saying you deserve all this until you call for the help of the Egyptian army and regret calling for the downfall of the military [regime]" (Mosireen Collective, 2012c).

9 Head of the public prosecution office.

10 Morsi was captured and detained by the military, led by his minister of defense at the time, Abdel Fattah El Sisi, current president of Egypt since June 2014.

11 The exception was in the case of First Lieutenant Mahmoud Alshinawi, who was popularly known as qnass el'ooyoon [the eyes' sniper].

6 The Power of the Shahadat: A Legitimate Arabyya
Feminist Methodology and a Strategy of Exposure
and Resistance

1 مؤسسة المرأة الجديدة.

2 نظرة للدراسات النسويّة.

3 On the second anniversary of the Revolution, January 25, 2013, 19 women were mob raped in Tahrir Square and the streets around it (Zaki & Abd Alhamid, 2014).

4   The population of Egypt is 101 million per the United Nations Population Fund (2019).

5   .ثورة المرأة العربية

6   .قوة ضد التحرش/الإعتداء الجنسي الجماعي

7   .خريطة التحرش الجنسي

8   .جوانا جوزيف

9   .بطلاتنا مش هيخلصو

10 Samira did not use the term "rape" in any of her shahadat. She maintained the use of kushoof el'uzryyah throughout.

11 .عار

12 .عزّا أو عرئ

13 .ثورة المرأة في العالم العربي

14 .كلنا ياسمين البرماوي

15 .قد تصل لجسدي لكنك أبداً لن تهزم روحي

16 Nadia Kamel is addressing one of the revolutionists/the Revolution's figures, Ahmad Maher, who was just released out of General El Sisi's political detentions, "from cage like cells in prisons to the country as a bigger cage, from the prison to the slums of social arrest" (Kamel, personal communication, February 15, 2017). She wanted to begin a conversation with Ahmad Maher on the question of "Did the Revolution fail?"

REFERENCES

aamiry-khasawnih, a. (2018). Four times "Egyptian Identity": Mural collaboration as dissent in times of crisis. *InVisibleCulture: An Electronic Journal for Visual Culture, 28*. https://ivc.lib.rochester.edu/four-times-egyptian-identity/

Abdelhadi, R., & Abdulhadi, R. (2002). Nomadic existence: Exile, gender and Palestine (an e-mail conversation between sisters). In G. E. Anzaldúa & A. Keating (Eds.), *This bridge we call home: Radical visions for transformation* (pp. 165–175). Routledge.

Abdel Hafeez, S. A. (2013, January 27). *Survivor of mass rape: This is what they did to me in liberation.* https://elaph.com/Web/news/2013/1/789221.html

Abdulhadi, F. (2006a). *The political role of Palestinian women in the 1930s.* Palestinian Women's Research & Documentation Center/UNESCO.

Abdulhadi, F. (2006b). *The political role of Palestinian women in the 1940s.* Palestinian Women's Research & Documentation Center/UNESCO.

Abdulhadi, F. (2009). *The political role of Palestinian women in 1950–1965.* Palestinian Women's Research & Documentation Center/UNESCO.

Abdulhadi, F. (2017, November 26). Quwatt al hikayah wa sihruha [The power and magic of story]. Masahat al hiwar [Space for dialogue]. *Al Safsaf Online.* http://www.al-safsaf.com/ال-عبد-قاسم-فيحاء-ها-د-سحر-وقوة-الحكاية/

Abouelnaga, S. (2015). Reconstructing gender in post-revolution Egypt. In M. El Said, L. Meari, & N. Pratt (Eds.), *Rethinking gender in revolution and resistance: Lessons from the Arab world* (pp. 35–58). Zed Books.

Abouelnaga, S. (2016). *Women in revolutionary Egypt: Gender and the new geographies of identity.* American University of Cairo.

Ahmed, L. (1992). *Women and gender in Islam: Historical roots of a modern debate.* Yale University Press.

Ahram Online. (2012, March 16). Activists organize solidarity with Samira Ibrahim. *Ahram Online.* http://english.ahram.org.eg/News/36912.aspx.

Ahsan Nas. (2013, June 22). *Yasmine El Baramawy: "Narrates her touching story about her experience of group rape."* [Video]. https://www.youtube.com/watch?v=YoNnGCtSGPI&t=172s

Akhbar El yom TV. (2012, September 6). *Public meeting* [Video]. https://www.youtube.com/watch?v=JZtEej5eB7A

Al-Ali, N. (2012). Gendering the Arab Spring. *Middle East Journal of Culture and Communication, 5*(1), 26–31.

Al-Ali, N. (2014). Reflections on (counter)revolutionary processes in Egypt. *Feminist Review, 106*, 122–128.

Alexander, A., & Bassiouny, M. (2014). *Bread, freedom, social justice: Workers and the Egyptian revolution.* Zed Books.

Al-Hassan Golley, N. (2004). Is feminism relevant to Arab women? *Third World Quarterly, 25*(3), 521–536. https://doi.org/10.1080/0143659042000191410

Almaany. (n.d.). The meanings: An online Arabic dictionary. *Almaany.* https://www.almaany.com/ar/dict/ar-ar/حكاية/

Al-Nakib, M. (2013). Disjunctive synthesis: Deleuze and Arab feminism. *Signs, 38*(2), 459–482. https://doi.org/10.1086/667220

al-Natour, M. (2012). The role of women in the Egyptian 25th January revolution. *Journal of International Women's Studies, 13*(5), 59–76.

Amar, P. (2013). Egypt. In P. Amar & V. Prashad (Eds.), *Dispatches from the Arab Spring: Understanding the new Middle East* (pp. 24–61). University of Minnesota Press.

Amar, P., & Prashad, V. (Eds.). (2013). *Dispatches from the Arab Spring: Understanding the new Middle East.* University of Minnesota Press.

Andeel, M. (n.d.). *Mada Masr: Andeel.* https://www.madamasr.com/en/contributor/andeel/

Anzaldúa, G. E. (1999). *Borderlands/La frontera: The new mestiza* (2nd ed.). Spinsters/Aunt Lute.

Badran, M. (2007). *Feminism beyond east and west: New gender talk and practice in global Islam.* Global Media Productions.

Badran, M. (2009). *Feminism in Islam: Secular and religious convergences.* Oneworld.

Badran, M. (2011, March 3). Egypt's revolution and the new feminism. *The Immanent Frame.* https://tif.ssrc.org/2011/03/03/egypts-revolution-and-the-new-feminism/

Baheth. (n.d.). Researcher: An online Arabic dictionary. *Baheth.* http://www.baheth.info/all.jsp?term=%D8%B4%D8%A7%D9%87%D8%AF.

Baker, M. (2013). Translation as an alternative space for political action. *Social Movement Studies, 12*(1), 23–47.

Baker, M. (2016). *Translating dissent: Voices from and with the Egyptian revolution.* Routledge.

Balba, A. (2013, January 31). *Interview with Reem Maged.* Interview by R. Maged. In O. Shoeb. *Baldna Bilmasri* [Television broadcast]. Egypt: OnTV.

Bayat, A. (2017). *Revolution without revolutionaries: Making sense of the Arab Spring.* Stanford University Press.

Carr, S. (2014, July 7). Sexual assault and the state: A history of violence. *Mada Masr.* https://madamasr.com/en/2014/07/07/feature/politics/sexual-assault-and-the-state-a-history-of-violence/

Castro, O., & Ergun, E. (2017). *Feminist translation studies: Local and transnational perspectives*. Routledge.

D'Isidoro, J. (Producer). (2019, February 20). Journalist Sharif Abdel Kouddous talks about U.S.-backed dictator Gen. Abdel Fattah el-Sisi's iron grip on Egypt. *Intercepted* [Audio podcast]. https://theintercept.com/2019/02/20/regime-change-we-can-believe-in-the-u-s-agenda-in-venezuela-haiti-and-egypt/

Delgado Bernal, D. (1998). Using a Chicana feminist epistemology in educational research. *Harvard Educational Review, 68*(4), 555–582.

Delgado Bernal, D., Burciaga, R., & Flores Carmona, J. (2012). Chicana/Latina testimonios: Mapping the methodological, pedagogical and political. *Equity & Excellence in Education, 45*(3), 363–372.

EIPR. (2011, March 16). *Virginity tests interview at EIPR offices with Rasha Abdulrahman.* https://858.ma/ANR/player/00:10:47.016

EIPR. (2012a, January 19). *Letter to the head of the medical union.* https://eipr.org/press/2012/01/رسالة-إلى-نقابة-الأطباء-لإصدار-قرار-بحظر-إجراء-فحوص-العذرية-الإجبارية

EIPR. (2012b, March 12). *We pledge to continue the pursuit of all involved in this crime and attempted cover-up: Military "virginity testing' verdict—not the last battle* [Press release]. https://eipr.org/en/press/2012/03/we-pledge-continue-pursuit-all-involved-crime-and-attempted-cover-military-virginity

EIPR. (2012c, December 24). *Lack of redress for women who underwent forced "virginity tests" challenged by Egyptian and international NGOs* [Press release]. https://eipr.org/en/press/2012/09/lack-redress-women-who-underwent-forced-virginity-tests-challenged-egyptian-and

EIPR. (2013a, January 29). *Operation anti-sexual harassment/assault condemns the attacks on women in Tahrir Square on Friday January 25th, the failure of political groups to secure the square and unprofessional media conduct* [Press release] https://eipr.org/en/press/2013/01/operation-anti-sexual-harassmentassault-condemns-attacks-women-tahrir-square-friday

EIPR. (2013b, December 13). *African commission declares "virginity tests" case admissible: Lack of accountability for violations in military prisons addressed in regional human rights mechanism* [Press release]. https://eipr.org/en/press/2013/12/african-commission-declares-"virginity-tests"-case-admissible-lack-accountability

EIPR. (2016, October 24). *The cessation court confirms criminal court verdict against ex-president Mohammed Morsi: A partial justice and waste of victims' rights* [Press release]. https://eipr.org/press/2016/10/تأييد-محكمة-النقض-لحكم-الجنايات-على-الرئيس-الأسبق-محمد-مرسي-في-قضية-الاتحادية-عدالة

El Baramawy, Y. [TEDx Talks]. (2013, December 2). *A stand against harassment: Yasmine El Baramawy at TEDxTandtaWoment* [Video]. https://www.youtube.com/watch?v=rrEgQyGwzds

El Baramawy, Y (2013, January 31). Interview with Reem Maged. *Baldna Bilmasri* [Television broadcast]. Egypt: OnTV.

El Saadawi, N. (1998). *The Nawal El Saadawi reader.* Zed Books.

El Said, M., Meari, L., & Pratt, N. (Eds.). (2015). *Rethinking gender in revolution and resistance: Lessons from the Arab world.* Zed Books.

Elsadda, H. (2011). Women's rights activism in post-Jan 25 Egypt: Combatting the shadow of the first lady syndrome in the Arab worlds. *Middle East Law and Governance, 3,* 84–93.

Elsadda, H., & Sabea, H. (2018). Introduction. Guest edited by Hoda Elsadda and Hanan Sabea. *Cairo Papers in Social Science: Oral History in Times of Change, 35*(1): 1–12.

El Nadeem. (n.d.). *El Nadeem Center for Rehabilitation of Victims of Torture and Violence* [Facebook page]. https://www.facebook.com/elnadeem/

Eladl, D. (2017). Fifty cartoons & more on women. *Farah Shafie.* https://farahshafie.com/blog/doaa-eladl-exhibition-book-review

El-Mahdi, R., & Marfleet, P. (2009). *Egypt: The moment of change.* Zed Books.

Fahim, M. [Magdy Fahim]. (2013, February 1). *Yasmine narrates the harassment incident she went through in Tahrir* [Video]. https://www.youtube.com/watch?v=vZVNosY-2DA

Fahmy, K. (2015, November 3). The long revolution: The Arab Spring was two centuries in the making. But is the Egyptian revolution any closer to ending the state's tyranny? *Aeon.* https://aeon.co/essays/how-the-egyptian-revolution-began-and-where-it-might-end

Fierros, C., & Delgado Bernal, D. (2016). *Vamos a pláticar:* The contours of *pláticas* as Chicana/Latina feminist methodology. *Chicana/Latina Studies: The Journal of MALCS, 15*(2), 98–121.

Flores Carmona, J. (2014). Cutting out their tongues: Mujeres' testimonios and the malintzin researcher. *Journal of Latino/Latin American Studies, 6*(2), 113–124.

Flores Carmona, J., Hamzeh, M., Bejarano, C., Hernández Sánchez, M., & El Ashmawi, Y. (2018). *Pláticas~testimonios:* Reimagining methodological borderlands for solidarity and resilience in academia. *Chicana/Latina Studies: The Journal of Mujeres Activas en Letras y Cambio Social (MALCS), 18*(1), 30–52.

Foda, Y. [OnTV]. (2012, December 6). *Interview with Akher Kalam* [Video]. https://www.youtube.com/watch?v=AXsjfrCouLI

Foxman, A. H. (2013, May 14). The contradiction of Samira Ibrahim. *Huffington Post.* https://www.huffpost.com/entry/the-contradiction-of-sami_b_2876719

Hafez, S. (2014). The revolution shall not pass through women's bodies: Egypt, uprising and gender politics. *Journal of North African Studies, 19*(2), 172–185.

Hamzeh, M. (2011). Deveiling body stories: Muslim girls negotiate visual, spatial, and ethical hijabs. *Race Ethnicity and Education, 14*(4), 481–506.

Hamzeh, M. (2012). *Pedagogies of deveiling: Muslim girls and the hijab discourse.* Information Age Press.

Hamzeh, M. (2018). Testimonios as methodology: Archiving, translating and theorizing Egyptian women's experiences of gendered violence in the January 25th Revolution. *Cairo Papers in Social Science: Oral History in Times of Change, 35*(1), 124–131.

Hamzeh, M., & Flores Carmona, J. (2019). Arabyyah and Mexicana co-teaching–learning testimonios of revolutionary women: A pedagogy of solidarity. *Educational Forum, 83*(3), 325–337.

Harassmap (n.d.). *Harassmap: Who we are.* https://harassmap.org/en/who-we-are

Hassan, M., & Magdy, D. (2018). Narrating gender in Egypt's public sphere: The archive of women's oral history. *Cairo Papers in Social Science: Oral History in Times of Change, 35*(1), 134–144.

Hasso, F. S., & Salime, Z. (2016). *Freedom without permission: Space and bodies in the Arab revolutions.* Duke University Press.

Hill Collins, P. (2017). Preface: On translation and intellectual activism. In O. Castro & E. Ergun (Eds.), *Feminist translation studies: Local and transnational perspectives* (pp. xi–xvi). Routledge.

Human Rights Watch (HRW). (2011, November 9). *Egypt: Military "virginity test" investigation a sham—Impunity highlights lack of independence of justice system* [Press release]. https://www.hrw.org/news/2011/11/09/egypt-military-virginity-test-investigation-sham

Hussein, A. (2012, March 12). "The future of Egyptian women is in danger"—Samira Ibrahim speaks out. *The Guardian.* https://www.theguardian.com/lifeandstyle/2012/mar/13/women-samira-ibrahim-egypt-virginity-tests

Ibrahim, S. (2011, December 28). *Interview with Reem Maged.* Interview by R. Maged. In O. Shoeb. *Baldna Bilmasri* [Television broadcast]. Egypt: OnTV.

Ibrahim, S. [Al-Nahar TV]. (2012a, March 16). *Samira Ibrahim: Winning battle to prevent virginity inspections* [Video]. https://www.dailymotion.com/video/x6txmkn

Ibrahim, S. (2012b, April 26). *Samira Ibrahim.* https://samiraibrahim.wordpress.com/2012/02/

I Saw Harassment (n.d.). *I Saw Harassment* [Facebook page]. https://www.facebook.com/pg/Shoft.Ta7rosh/about/?ref=page_internal

Jackson, A. Y., & Mazzei, L. A. (2012). *Thinking with theory in qualitative research: Viewing data across multiple perspectives.* Routledge.

Jackson, A. Y., & Mazzei, L. A. (2013). Plugging one text into another: Thinking with theory in qualitative research, *Qualitative Inquiry, 19*(4), 261–271.

Kamal, H. (2016). A century of Egyptian women's demands: The four waves of the Egyptian feminist movement In S. Takhar (Ed.), *Gender and race matter: Global perspectives on being a woman.* (pp. 3–22). Emerald Insight.

Khaled, M. [XYZcreation]. (2017, February 9). *The thread and the wall* [Video]. https://www.youtube.com/watch?v=906dnBWVSr8

Latina Feminist Group. (2001). *Telling to live: Latina feminist testimonio.* Duke University Press.

Leavy, P., & Harris, A. (2019). *Contemporary feminist research from theory to practice.* Guilford Press.

Levison, B. (Producer), & Reticker, G. (Director). (2015). *The Trials of Spring* [Motion picture]. Fork Films.

Maajim (n.d.). Dictionaries: An online dictionary of classical Arabic dictionaries. *Maajim.* https://www.maajim.com/dictionary/العرب20%لسان/1/شهد.

Mada Masr (2018, February 11). 858: Archiving as a tool of resistance. *Mada Masr.* https://madamasr.com/en/2018/02/11/feature/culture/858-archiving-as-a-tool-of-resistance/

Meari, L. (2014). Sumud: A philosophy of confronting interrogation in colonial prisons. *South Atlantic Quarterly, 113*(31), 548–578.

Mikhael, R. [Rafeek Mikhael]. (2011, December 19). شهادة غادة كمال عن أحداث فض إعتصام مجلس الوزراء بالقوة [Video]. https://www.youtube.com/watch?v=89HWDWxm-Og

Mernissi, F. (1991). *The veil and the male elite: A feminist interpretation of women's rights in Islam.* (M. J. Lakeland, Trans.). Perseus.

Mernissi, F. (1997). *The forgotten queens of Islam.* (M. J. Lakeland, Trans.). University of Minnesota Press.

Moghadam, V. (2013). What is democracy? Promises and perils of the Arab Spring. *Current Sociology, 61*(4): 393–408.

Mohanty, C. T. (2013). Transnational feminist crossings: On neoliberalism and radical critique. *Signs: Journal of Women in Culture and Society, 38*(4), 967–991.

Moraga, C. (2002). Theory in the flesh. In C. Moraga & G. Anzaldúa (Eds.), *This bridge called my back: Writings by radical women of color* (p. 21). Aunt Lute Press.

Moraga, C., & Anzaldúa, G. (Eds.). (2002). *This bridge called my back: Writings by radical women of color.* Aunt Lute Press.

Mosireen Collective. (2012a, November 26). *Mona Seif: addakhylyya fi 'ahd: Morsi's interior ministry* [Video]. https://www.youtube.com/watch?v=UFtgogR1Mmo

Mosireen Collective. (2012b, November 30). *Tahrir: Safe zone for all* [Video]. https://www.youtube.com/watch?v=oQhoaWu3jX8

Mosireen Collective. (2012c, December 13). *Shuhood al itihhadyya, Ola Shahba* [Video]. https://www.youtube.com/watch?v=Bn9RcJgmgCU

Mostafa, D. S. (2015). Introduction: Egyptian women, revolution, and protest culture. *Journal for Cultural Research, 19*(2), 118–129. https://doi.org/10.108 0/14797585.2014.982916

Naber, N. (2011, February 11). Imperial feminism, Islamophobia, and the Egyptian Revolution. *Jadaliyyah.* http://www.jadaliyya.com/pages/index/616/ imperial-feminism-islamophobia-andthe-egyptian-revolution

Naber, N., & Said, A. (2016). The cry for human rights: Violence, transition, and the Egyptian revolution. *Humanity: An International Journal of Human Rights, Humanitarianism, and Development, 7*(1), 71–90.

Nagar, R. (2014). *Muddying the waters: Coauthoring feminisms across scholarship and activism.* University of Illinois Press.

Nazra for Feminist Studies. (2012, March 12). *We pledge to continue the pursuit of all involved in this crime and attempted cover-up: Military "virginity testing" verdict—not the last battle.* https://nazra.org/en/2012/03/military-virginity-testing-verdict-not-last-battle

Nazra for Feminist Studies. (2013, January 23). *Testimony of a survivor from group rape in the vicinity of Tahrir Square.* https://nazra.org/en/2013/01/testimony-survival-gang-rape-tahrir-square-vicinity

New Woman Foundation. (2012, December 3). *Testimony of group rape case in Mohammad Mahmood street.* http://nwrcegypt.org/-شهادة-حالة-اغتصاب-جماعي /في-محمد-محمود

OpAntiSH. (n.d.). *Operation Anti-Sexual Harassment/Assault* [Facebook page]. https://www.facebook.com/opantish

Reyes, K., & Rodríguez, J. (2012). Testimonio: Origins, terms, and resources. *Equity & Excellence in Education, 45*(3), 525–538.

Rosa Luxemburg Congress [Rosa-Luxemburg-Stiftung]. (2012, February 17). *Arab Revolt: Opportunities and limits of civil disobedience* [Video]. https://www. youtube.com/watch?v=4Hqe7fpg_xM

Saa'd, M. [MediaMasrTV14]. (2013, February 1). *A brave girl tells the details of her rape in Tahrir* [Video]. https://www.youtube.com/watch?v=KVRlvts-JEg

Said, A. (2011). After the revolution. *Amnesty International, 38*(2), 12–21.

Said, O. (2015). Qira'a fi hukom qadyat 'al itihhadyyah' siyasi wa laysa munssifan. *Mada Masr.* https://madamasr.com/ar/2015/04/22/feature/-سياسة/قراءة-في /حكم-قضية-الاتحادية-سياسي-ولي

Santaemilia, J. (2017). A corpus-based analysis of terminology in gender and translation research: A case of feminist translation. In O. Castro & E. Ergun (Eds.), *Feminist translation studies: Local and transnational perspectives* (pp. 25–28). Routledge.

Schifrin, N. (2016, February 12). Can Egyptian women start a revolution against sexual violence? *PBS News Hour.* https://www.pbs.org/newshour/show/can-egyptian-women-start-a-revolution-against-sexual-violence

Seikaly, S. (2013, January 27). The meaning of revolution: On Samira Ibrahim. *Jadaliyyah.* http://www.jadaliyya.com/Details/27915/The-Meaning-of-Revolution-On-Samira-Ibrahim

Shewy Media. (2011, December 18). *The testimony of Ghada Kamal after the army attacked her on December 16* [Video]. https://www.youtube.com/watch?v=Rgq4prhzots

Shorbagy, M. (2007). Understanding kefaya: The new politics in Egypt. *Arab Studies Quarterly, 29*(1), 39–60.

tahrirDiary (2011a, March 16). *Salwa Al Husseini Judah: Arrested by the military on March 9* [Video]. https://www.youtube.com/watch?v=CUcS78w8gss

tahrirDiary. (2011b, November 15). *Samira & the army: A story of an Egyptian girl* [Video]. https://www.youtube.com/watch?v=c29CAXR141s

Theron, C. (2012, April 18). Samira Ibrahim: Plaintiff. *Time.* http://content.time.com/time/specials/packages/article/0,28804,2111975_2111976_2111959,00.html

Tissot, D. (2017). Transnational feminist solidarities and the ethics of translation In O. Castro & E. Ergun (Eds), *Feminist translation studies: Local and transnational perspectives* (pp. 29–41). Routledge.

Trinidad Galván, R. (2014). Chicana/Latin American feminist epistemologies of the Global South (within and outside the North): Decolonizing *el conocimiento* and creating global alliances. *Journal of Latino/Latin American Studies, 6*(2), 135–140.

United Nations Population Fund (2019). *World population dashboard: Egypt.* https://www.unfpa.org/data/world-population/EG

Wadud, A. (1999). *Qur'an and women: Rereading the sacred text from a woman's perspective.* Oxford University Press.

Yousef, B. [Albernameg]. (2012, February 11). *Samir Ibrahim with Basem Yousef on Elbrnameg Program, OnTV* [Video]. https://www.youtube.com/watch?v=Gv3v9oWxZKU

Zaki, H., & Abd Alhamid, D. (2014, July 9). Women as fair game in the public sphere: A critical introduction for understanding sexual violence and methods of resistance. *Jadaliyya.* https://www.jadaliyya.com/Details/30930/Women-As-Fair-Game-in-the Public-Sphere-A-Critical-Introduction-for-Understanding-Sexual Violence-and-Methods-of-Resistance

INDEX